By reading this document, the reader agrees that under no circumstances is the author responsible for any losses, direct or indirect, which are incurred as a result of the use of the information contained within this document, including, but not limited to, — errors, omissions, or inaccuracies.

Table of Contents

MINDFULNESS MEDITATION FOR ANXIETY:

THE COMPLETE GUIDE TO HELP YOU FIGHT ANXIETY AND DEPRESSION, OVERCOME PANIC ATTACKS, HAVE A DEEP SLEEP AND REDUCE STRESS IN YOUR DAILY LIFE

Introduction

Anxiety is a feeling of worry or fear that normally apprehends you before you confront something that you consider challenging; for instance, an interview, test or examination. Having such feelings is considered to be normal and a part of life. Actually, anxiety in moderation is actually good as it enables you to be focused, stay alert, and to be able to handle situations head on. The problem comes in when these feelings make you unable to sleep or otherwise function normally. This means that anxiety is seen to be out of hand when feelings such as worry or fear do not subside and continue to exist even without any particular cause or reason. This then becomes a serious condition that makes you unable to continue with your daily routine.

On the other hand, panic attacks are usually as a result of having extremely heightened anxiety. The attack might last for a few minutes or even go on for some hours but without treatment, prolonged and frequent panic attacks can be very disabling. The physical symptoms might be caused by your body getting into a fight or flight mode in response to something you assume to be a threat. Your body will, therefore, try to take in more oxygen and, therefore, your breathing will quicken. Your body will also release some hormones such as adrenaline, which will make your muscles to tense up and your heart to beat faster.

Even with the basic understanding of what anxiety is about, it is important to understand that anxiety is not just a one size fits all kind of problem; different people experience it differently. There are various types of anxiety disorders. Below are some of the most common anxiety disorders.

Panic disorder

This is a type of anxiety disorder where you experience sudden or brief attacks of intense apprehension and terror that leads to confusion, difficulty breathing, shaking, nausea, and dizziness. Other symptoms may include chest pain, sweating, a feeling of chocking and unusually strong and irregular heartbeats, which may make you to feel as though you are having a heart attack or you are going crazy. Panic attacks usually rise instantly and peak after about 10 minutes after which they may last for some hours. A panic attack frequently occurs after prolonged stress or frightening events but sometimes they might arise with no specific trigger.

Stress

We had positive considerations, yet they didn't really help. Our inward voice regularly wrecks our endeavors to win throughout everyday life. We get diverted and overlook, or stress over what might occur. Or then again, question executes any great that would happen to it. Would you be able to identify with this? Utilizing a baseball allegory, this is strike one.

If you are attempting to produce the get up and go to push ahead as a result of negative things, the time has come to make a positive move. You might haul around sentiments from a mistake, a disappointment, or a negative picture from an earlier time which is hindering you. If that is the situation, remember it, manage it helpfully, and choose to roll out a positive improvement in your reasoning.

Presently, what we are discussing here is the thing that numerous individuals allude to as being stuck, lacking inspiration, feeling stuck, or concentrating on negative feelings. A situation that is normally, pretty much, a transient event. Assuming, in any case, you are managing a worry that goes a lot further than this, don't spare a moment to make a sound move and request help from a certified source.

Negative sentiments and pictures that putrefy and are continually returned to can uniquely slow down endeavors to start crisp and push ahead. Both negative and positive mental self-portraits are ground-breaking, and endeavoring to live with both at the same time is a conflict of intellectual prowess that essentially doesn't work. Consider it one counteracting the other.

A cognizant decision to discharge negative considerations and pictures must be made so as to take into consideration new and positive encounters to happen. Doing this enables you to relinquish restricting convictions and to change your point of view. It, as a rule, expects you to step outside your usual range of familiarity - yet that is the place most achievement truly grabs hold.

In this book you can find information that can help you finding solutions to your anxiety and stress's problems. I will explain you everything that is essential to achieve your goal of dealing with anxiety and stress both at your home and at work.

Although this book is not a substitute for medical advice, it is a product of my experiences. You will be able to relate with these experiences in your everyday life. I really understand how easy it is to go through life, living in a constant state of anxiety, or letting your stress and worries drag you down. So, I want this book to help you overcome anxiety, cut yourself off from these burdens and finally live a happier life.

In this book you will get a lot of information. However, your success depends on how you will apply them. Are you willing to make the first step? Or you will procrastinate until anxiety will eat you up from inside, or stress will become unbearable? Since you made the choice to get this book, I believe you will make the right step and I am confident that you will not procrastinate!

You need to take immediate action. Use this book as your guide to change your life today.

Part 1. Meditation for Anxiety and Stress Relief

Chapter 1.   Origin of Meditation

Meditation has a long and rich history. This mental and physical wellness art is dated as far back as some of the old civilizations and religions. Meditation is closely interlinked to religion in many of the places where it is traditionally practiced and may have its roots in religion.

Meditation techniques were employed for the attainment of a higher purpose in the pursuit of divine perfection and to bring one closer to the creator. Research has it that the earliest evidence of meditation is in Hindu scriptural texts. It is from these beginnings that other forms of meditation developed in Asia and the Orient. In the 5th and 6th centuries, meditation has been adopted by Taoists in China and Hindus, Jains, and Buddhists in India.

In Islam, Sufism, and Dhikr, meditation is practiced through word repetitions, chants, movements, and controlled breathing. In the West, Christian meditation picked up around the sixth century during Bible readings among Benedictine monks. Modern forms of meditation that most of us practice today appeared in India in the 1950s as secular forms of meditation techniques that are more geared toward the reduction of stress, self-improvement, and relaxation. The modern forms of meditation do not focus on spirituality.

Meditation was used by these religions as techniques for bringing practitioners closer to God, for the closer one was to

God, the more peaceful they were and the more clarity of mind they attained. With this brief history and knowledge of meditation, let us look at the different types and techniques of meditation practiced around the world in the next section.

Meditation has a long history chiefly in the Buddhism tradition. In India, meditation dates back to more than 5000 years. Between 2000 and 3000 BC, discoveries of Vedic Meditation texts on Hindu texts increased the interest in meditation. During the 1000 BC, ancient Indians found the Qi Gong, which was a meditative motion that later became Tai Chi. The development of Buddhism in 588 BC is attributable to Buddha's meditation. From the Buddhism notion, meditation is a technique that seeks to free the mind from any suffering. The men who introduced the practice are the yogis. They meditated as a way to train their bodies and minds to achieve wellness. One of the Indian Yogis, known as Patanjali, defined meditation as a process of self-realization. Patanjali wrote the yoga techniques applicable today, with the seventh stage being meditation. Meditation paved the way for Yoga, which continued to spread gradually in China, Tibet, and India.

In the West, the monks were the first people to meditate, which was 200 AC. The monks practiced meditation as a way to grower closer to God. Later on, several Jewish groups meditated regularly to grow spiritually. In the 1500s, St. Theresa favored the practice of meditation, and it grew extensively during that period. However, the Christian religion did not embrace the concept entirely. The growth of meditation in the U.S mostly gained precedence in the 1800s when Asian priests presented the ideas on meditation during a religious leaders' meeting. Later in the 1960s, the Beatles started practicing meditation leading to the rapid growth of the practice in the West. In recent years, meditation is gaining full acceptance in science and healthcare. More people are viewing it trendy and as a part of mental detox. Resultantly, millions of young and older people have been meditating, not only as a stress-reliever but also for relaxation.

So, what is meditation? In simple terms, meditation is the concept of being peaceful, silent, and meditative. Buddha once said meditation is when a mirror does not reflect anything. The Latin words, *meditari*, which is to think and *mederi*, which is to heal, make up the word meditation. Originally, meditation is from the Sanskrit term '*Medha*,' meaning wisdom. It also has origins from the phrase *shamatha*, meaning relaxation or calmness. From the two derivations, it is clear that meditation makes your mind quiet, leading one to have contact with the self or true identity.

Consequently, you will experience bliss, peace, and joy. Through meditation, you understand your mind and learn ways to transform any negative thoughts into positive thoughts. For successful meditation, you will need to have attitudes such as patience, trust, non-judgmental, letting go, and acceptance.

Scientifically, research on medication was evident in 1963. James Funderburk created a collection of studies on meditation under the guidance of Swami Rama. In fact, western scientists studied Swami Rama as the first yogis. While scientists had concluded that most of the bodily processes are involuntary, Rama proved them otherwise. He demonstrated his innate abilities to control some of his physical processes voluntarily. Rama controlled some of the processes, such as body temperature, blood pressure, and heartbeat. Through meditation, he could change his heartbeat while in a motionless posture. Rama could also use his mind to contract and dilate his blood vessels, consequently affecting his skin temperatures. Further, Rama could get his brain to a deep sleep while he remained conscious of his surroundings. Many of his demonstrations triggered the scientific community to study more about meditation and its impacts on the body.

In the decades that followed, scientific studies increased in quality and quantity. Practitioners within other traditions such as the Tibetan Lamas and the Zen monks demonstrated and studied the processes of mind over the body. In the 1970s, Dr. Herbert Benson studied the impact of meditation at Harvard University. His contribution enhanced the acknowledgment of meditation in healthcare. In the 21st century, meditation has mostly become a secularized concept. However, spiritual meditation is still in existence, especially in Hinduism. The wide-ranging benefits on overall wellness, mind, and body are attributable to the increasing popularity of meditation.

In recent years, meditation has proved to be useful in stress management and enhancement of mindfulness. Meditation leads to mindfulness, which consists of being constantly aware of your mind. During meditation, disruptive thoughts may emerge, but the driving purpose of its use is to push them away. A clear mind is the key to embracing new ideas and perspective and with one, it is possible to handle stressful situations and solve any issue. Although meditation hails predominantly from India, it is a practice that is not solely associated with Buddhism. Human beings have a mindful nature and meditation takes a significant role in human capacity. Through mindfulness, people are not only better able to cope and process life events, but also, more capable of remaining stable and not reacting to the external environment. Meditation allows one to possess a clear mind, generate energy, and promote joy within their own life.

The process of meditation is three-fold, leading to a consciousness state that brings about clarity and serenity. The first stage is dealing with our 'normal' mind, which is, in reality, abnormal. The reason one can view the mind as strange is the uncontrolled reaction to sensory stimuli. Bouncing from thoughts to thoughts is the nature of almost all humans of sound mind. As discussed in the introduction, our minds are like rooms full of clamoring monkeys, the noise and the jumping up and down define how our thoughts are structured. This simple diagram is an actual illustration of our rational minds at every moment.

The second phase of meditation is concentration, which is the gradual process of gaining control of the mind. Concentration involves picking a subject or an object and focusing on it exclusively without diversifying your mind. Without active attention, meditation is impossible. The illustration below is that of a concentrating mind.

The last stage is meditation, characterized by unbroken attention. When you concentrate without distractions, the concentration on the meditation object deepens spontaneously and effortlessly. At this final stage, your mind unites with the object of meditation. You get to the contemplation stage, which is the state of utmost consciousness. Being in a state of consciousness 'separates' us from the rest of the universe. Initially, this deep sense of peace might be challenging to achieve. You will need to practice the procedures repeatedly and slowly to achieve the serenity you desire.

The process of meditation is dependent on a few aspects that play a crucial role in the determination of how effective the eventual outcomes. When preparing for meditation, one needs to consider the immediate environment as a critical factor towards achieving the desired end goal. Meditation is most effective when in a serene, quiet surrounding away from the distractions of life. The process of preparing for meditation may require a keen focus on the calmness of the surroundings and the comfort within which the body and mind can enter into a space of complete relaxation. If in a room, ensure that the place is well-ventilated to allow for the circulation of fresh air into the room. Breathing is a critical part of the process of meditation, which means that a ventilated setting is a necessity.

The other option would be to enroll in a yoga studio, where such factors are often put into consideration. Then decide on which techniques work best for you.

This book offers a wide range of techniques to determine from before deciding on what works best. You may need to engage a meditation specialist if unsure of what may work best for you. The next critical consideration should be the consideration of how to undertake specific movements and postures when engaging in the meditation process. Essentially, it is worth noting that particular positions and movement may require extreme stretches, which may lead to injuries if not well-choreographed. Understanding the choreography in each of the poses and motions will also enhance the possibility of achieving the best results from the meditation process. Consulting a specialist before beginning the process may be useful, especially when engaging in the highly physical meditation techniques such as Yoga. On the same note having a YouTube tutorial or other sources of information can help you begin the process of meditation from the point of knowledge.

People must understand that meditation is not an escapist approach when faced with challenges. In fact, it is the opposite; meditation allows you to confront problems and to demystify any misconceptions about a situation. It mainly involves settling one experience in an objective way to achieve a calm state of mind. With the many complexities in the modern society, meditation can be an ideal solution. The process is straightforward because the object of meditation can be anything. You only need to be away from distractions and focus on concentration.

If you want to start the practice of meditation today, thousands of online guides can prove resourceful. You only need whether you are a beginner or an expert in meditation; the different guides have stipulated minutes to help your mind relax. Furthermore, you can meditate successfully without following specific guides. You will only need a quiet place, the right posture, and an object of meditation.

Practicing Meditation

The word 'meditation' originates from the Latin word *meditatio*, which means to think, ponder, or contemplate.

It is a method of deep relaxation that rests the mind and, in turn, the body.

Simply put, meditation is a peace of mind!

Meditation aims to achieve self-regulation of the mind by using the various meditation techniques for relaxation, mental clarity, and building positive internal energy. It is this end that helps to manage health problems, like anxiety, depression, and high blood pressure.

The body is nourished and healed through rest. You achieve deep relaxation through meditation; therefore, it is great for rejuvenating the body to leave you well and mentally serene. Research has shown that the degree of rest achieved when one is meditating is greater than that harnessed from sleep. The findings are incredible. Twenty minutes of deep meditation has been equated to seven hours of sleep!

The desired goal of mental clarity, positivity, and peace is reached through the regular practice of meditative techniques. For the maximum harvest of the benefits, be committed to this art. Over time, your body will get into a rhythm and in tune for inner peace.

Types and Techniques of Meditation

There are many different types and techniques of meditation that we shall not be able to cover everything. Meditative techniques are in the hundreds but are all linked by the common thread of aiming at achieving inner peace for the practitioner.

First and foremost, all meditative practices engage in mind-control techniques as a way to achieve relaxation and peace. Second, there are postures and body movements that are found in all forms of meditation. These two traits are evident in all meditative practices pointing to a common goal for all of them.

Meditation helps to relieve our bodies and minds of the toxic effects of stress. It relaxes us and brings the peace of mind that we all yearn for. Before you pick up one form of meditation or another, it is important to do your research and learn as much as you can about them. Interrogate yourself. Find out and decide what your meditative goals are or would be to help you pick up the right technique for you.

In some cases, you will need to get a teacher or join a meditation school for the right advice, coaching, and mentorship in taking up meditation. There are types of meditative practices that cannot be performed by beginners, people with certain conditions or illnesses, or older people, for example. Seeking the right information will guide you to the right technique. You must take on a meditative practice that will fit your lifestyle. Meditation requires consistency, regularity, discipline, and high commitment for one to realize the desired fruits. With the many types of meditation in existence, we can generally categorize meditation as follows:

1. Concentrative Meditation: In concentrative meditation, the mind is directed to a particular object, chant/mantra, sound, or sensation. The practitioner will focus their mind and energy on a focal point of their choosing that best works for them to clear and calm their minds and bodies. This type of meditation is good for beginners.

2. Mindfulness Meditation: This type of meditation does not rely on focusing the mind on an object but relies on feelings, sensations, emotions and thought patterns to achieve a meditative state. These are more advanced types of meditation that are not for everyone, especially beginners:

3. Buddhist Meditation: Zen Meditation (Zazen): Zazen is Japanese meaning "seated Zen" or "seated meditation," referring to the form of Zen meditation practiced while sitting. Zazen originates from Chinese Zen Buddhism. It is done while seated on the floor, usually on a mat, with crossed legs. This was traditionally done in the lotus or half-lotus position. For the mind, Zazen employs two techniques:

   - Focus on breathing. The practitioner will pay attention to the inhalation and exhalation while silently counting down with every breath and back.

- Shikantaza. Here, there is no specific object of meditation. One remains in the moment being aware of what goes through their mind and what passes around.

1. Vipassana Meditation: Vipassana means clear seeing or insight and is a Buddhist type of meditation. It is ideal for mental discovery and awareness. It starts with mindfulness of breath to stabilize and focus the mind (focused-mind meditation), then it moves to develop clarity of awareness of bodily sensations and mental phenomena. Sit on the floor, legs crossed, with a straight back.

2. Mindfulness Meditation: Mindfulness meditation combines practices from various Buddhist meditation practices. It is widely employed in hospitals and other health benefits as a form of treatment. Here, the practitioner will focus on the moment while not losing awareness of thoughts and emotions experienced.

3. Religious/Spiritual Meditation. These are meditative practices that are practiced among different religions. Remember that spirituality is one avenue for achieving peace of mind and relaxation. Here, meditation and prayer are combined to achieve spiritual development by the reflection of God's Word. Meditation is a communion with the self with the aim of spiritual development or divinity.

Meditation in religion is practiced for peace of mind by steadying and focusing it on giving the practitioner the ability for divine insight. A practitioner of Christian meditation said that God is sought through the study of scripture, but through meditation, He is found. There are forms of meditative practices in almost all religions, which prove the close link between spirituality and meditation.

Sufism meditative practices are some of the most elaborate of religious meditation. Practitioners get into a rhythm of chanting and movement that eventually transports participants into a spiritual realm. In Christianity, there are examples with the Catholics and Orthodox sects that have mantras or repetitive prayers.

4. Metta Meditation. It is also referred to as loving-kindness meditation and has its roots in Tibet. This meditative form enhances empathy and compassion to make one more loving to self and others. The practitioner will sit and close their eyes, then generate feelings of kindness and compassion in their mind toward themselves then progress to others. Just like the name suggests, this type of meditation aims at creating harmony with one's surroundings. Treat all things with

kindness, and the rewards are happiness and compassion for you. You emit happiness, and the world bounces it back to you.

5. Hindu Meditations: Vedic and Yogic forms of meditation are Hindu forms and are classified as follows:

6. Mantra Meditation. Mantra involves the repetition of a word or phrase to focus on one's mind.

7. Transcendental Meditation. Transcendental techniques aim at opening the mind.

8. Yoga Meditation. Yoga means "union," and it has many types. Yoga combines mind relaxing and focusing on practices with stretching movements and postures. Of all the meditative practices, yoga is the most popular of the secular forms of meditation and has the most following for nonreligious or spiritual meditation. You will find that most people who meditate are practicing one form of yoga or another.

How then do we use these techniques for self-improvement and relaxation? Let us first know the benefits of meditation.

Benefits of Meditation

There are several benefits apart from the ones we have discussed in the preceding sections. It is no wonder then that meditation is being promoted as an alternative to clinical treatment for the cure and management of several health conditions and general wellbeing. Meditation leads the body to change. Cells in the body are injected with more energy resulting in peace, happiness, and motivation as the energy levels in the body are boosted.

Below are the benefits of meditative practices:

- Meditation reverses or reduces the production of stress hormones (adrenaline) by creating calmness and eradicating anxiety to prevent chronic stress. With controlled or regulated stress hormones, the body is more relaxed.

- It is good for managing blood pressure and other heart diseases or conditions since the heart rate and breathing are slowed down. When we are not stressed, worried, or anxious, the heart rate is slow; therefore, the blood pressure is also low. Meditation can help greatly with conditions like high blood pressure since it works to create calmness and relaxation.

- Boosts the immune system and slows aging as a result of less production of adrenaline by the body. The immune system is boosted since one ends up being healthier as a result of the suppression of destructive stress chemicals.

- Meditation brings clarity of the mind, and creativity is enhanced. With a relaxed mind, one is sure to be more creative and productive.

- Meditative techniques advocate for a pure life, and in fact, meditation aims to attain purity akin to the higher being, so practitioners find themselves quitting poisonous habits, like smoking, drug abuse, and alcohol consumption.

- Brain functioning is greatly improved through the boosting of psychological creativity, a better memory, and a settled, relaxed mind.

- Meditation makes you happier since your mind and body feel better. A relaxed person has no worries and will be a happier person.

- You will sleep better since you are relaxed, enabling you to have more rest and better rest to face the day and tasks that you are faced with.

- Meditation reduces how fast we age through mental and physical exercise. People who meditate have a slower aging process. Stress hormones hasten aging while meditation is known to halt or significantly reduce their production.

- Meditation reduces or eliminates stress. Meditation practice is a calm and happy individual who is essentially immune to the effects of stress.

- A relaxed and happier person has the benefit of a better functioning body. Immunity is boosted, and diseases are kept at bay.

- When one embraces meditation with all its tenets and understands it, they hold life to a greater value since they learn the true meaning and purpose of living.

- Meditative exercises improve metabolism and help regulate weight by fighting obesity.
- Meditation helps you feel more connected and in tune with yourself.
- Meditation brings emotional balance and harmony.
- Personal transformation is inevitable with meditation. You end up being a new person.

It is recommended that you meditate at least once a day for optimal results. Dawn meditation is highly recommended, usually between 3:00 a.m. and 6:00 a.m. Dawn meditation is considered more beneficial as you tend to be more alert and well-rested after your sleep. The environment is also quiet and ideal for meditation. In the next part, we shall learn how to use meditation to reduce stress in your life.

How to Reduce Stress by Meditating

So, what is stress? Stress is the body's way of responding to pressure that may be exerted on it physically or psychologically. Stress is caused when the body releases stress chemicals, usually adrenaline, into the blood to combat whatever pressure it is confronted with. Stress can be classified as follows:

- Survival stress. This is the stress that we face when we are confronted by dangerous situations where you feel that physical harm is imminent. It is here where we have a fight-and-flight response to fight stress.

- Internal stress. This is stress caused by worries over things that are out of your control. Simply put, internal stress is self-imposed stress that can be avoided by not giving yourself so much pressure over things that are beyond you.

- Environmental stress. This is stress caused by factors in your surroundings, like noise. Stay away from environmental stress triggers, and you will have a happy life.

- Tiredness. This type of stress is caused by fatigue, which usually accumulates over a long period due to such things as overworking.

Stress is an inescapable part of life, and sooner or later, we experience it. What we need to do is learn how to manage it so that it does not overwhelm us and take over our lives. Stress is not an entirely bad thing as it can enhance our alertness and concentration. However, in excess, it is very unhealthy.

Symptoms of Stress

How do you know if you are stressed? The following are some signs that will let you know if you are stressed.

Cognitive symptoms:

- Problems remembering things
- Low concentration
- High anxiety

- Constant worry

Emotional symptoms:

- Being moody
- Highly irritable and angry
- Loneliness and reclusion
- Sadness

Physical symptoms:

- Low libido
- Aches and pain
- High heart rate
- Dizziness

Behavioral symptoms:

- Eating disorders (bingeing or self-starving)
- Lack of sleep
- Substance abuse
- Nervousness

Causes of Stress

External causes:

- Major life changes (divorce, chronic illness, the death of a loved one)
- Work burden
- Financial problems

- Trauma

Internal causes:

- Constant worry
- Negativity and pessimism
- Fear and anxiety
- Unrealistic expectations

Side Effects of Stress

Stress can cause serious health and social problems if it is not dealt with immediately and well. Here are some of the side effects of stress:

- Mental disorders, like depression and anxiety
- Weight problems, such as obesity
- Problems with menstrual cycles
- Skin and hair problems (acne, hair loss, etc.)
- Sexual dysfunction
- Gastrointestinal problems, like ulcerative colitis

Meditation and Stress Management

Meditation has been proven as a stress reliever and is being embraced by many for relaxation. Stress relief needs both mental and physical relaxation, and meditation provides that. To understand why meditation is so helpful in reducing stress, we should know what it takes to relax:

- Deep breathing. Deep breathing is a quick and sure way of deflating stress from your system. This is a simple technique with far-reaching positive consequences in keeping stress in check.

- Balancing the nervous system. For the body to function optimally, the nervous system must be at equilibrium. You must be at peace mentally. Stress destabilizes this balance, and the only way to stead your system is by relaxation. A state of profound serenity of the nervous system is the counter to stress.

- Yoga: Yoga is a series of steady movement and stationary poses combined with deep breathing. Yoga reduces stress and improves flexibility, strength, balance, and stamina if practiced regularly. Almost all types of yoga are beneficial for stress and anxiety relief as they combine steady movement, deep breathing, and stretching. You may try the following types:

- Satyananda. This is a traditional form of yoga that uses meditation, gentle poses, and deep relaxation and is ideal for those who want to start practicing for stress and anxiety relief.

- Hatha Yoga. This is also a gentle form that is ideal for you to ease your way into practice.

- Power Yoga. Power yoga is more advanced and is for those who are already familiar with the basics. It is more intense, and the focus is on fitness. This is ideal for those seeking relaxation and stimulation.

- Tai Chi. Tai Chi is a mellow form of meditation suited for everyone. It is especially good for the elderly recovering from injuries and illnesses common with those of advanced age. It is a series of slow body movements, emphasizing concentration, circulation of energy through the body, and relaxation while focusing on breathing.

For you to effectively deal with stress and anxiety through meditation, it is important to be consistent in practicing whichever type of meditation you settle for. Make it part of your life. Practice it regularly until it becomes second nature. Here is what you need to do for a successful stress-relieving meditation experience:

- Get a quiet, serene place for your meditation exercise; this can be anywhere as long as it has no interference. It can be in your backyard, living room, in a park, etc.
- Assume a comfortable posture, whether seated, standing, or lying down. Start tuning your mind to the here and now. Focus and concentrate.
- In the posture with eyes closed, take a slow deep breath and relax your body as you do this. Get into an inhaling and exhaling rhythm.

- Clear your mind of distracting thoughts and concentrate on your meditation. Pay attention to your breathing, and concentrate on that only as you relax.

- Channel your mind to happy thoughts of a happy place you have been, or just concentrate on the present while listening to your breathing. Push out unwanted thoughts that may come your way.

- Keep your eyes closed, take deep breaths, and imagine your body relaxing. Keep doing this until you are completely relaxed.

Imagine a life of reduced anxiety and stress. Isn't that what we all want? By following the advice and tips discussed above, you will be able to effectively kick out stress from your life and remain a happy and relaxed individual. Whenever stress is left to get out of control, depression sets in. Depression is a condition that is directly linked to the mismanagement of stress. Depression is an extreme form of stress. Let us understand what depression is and how meditation can help in its relief.

Meditation, used properly, is one of the most effective tools for reducing an individual's anxiety and panic. It refers to various exercises that involve sitting and focusing on one's own breath or a nearby object. Meditation has proved useful in alleviating numerous symptoms of anxiety.

As shown by research, meditation can help individuals gain control of their physical tension and promote calmer, thoughtful reactions. During meditation, the heart beats at a slower pace, which lowers blood pressure, thus subsequently reducing anxiety and allowing the person to better cope with their anxiety.

Additionally, meditation has proven to drastically improve one's ability to control anxious thoughts, that would once be able to trigger a panicked response. Therefore, instead of allowing one's negative thoughts and emotions to consume them and dictate how they respond to various situations, people can learn how to manage their emotions and respond in a positive way when dealing with stressful situations.

When we panic, we let the irrational thoughts and emotions that we are feeling control the way we respond to the situation. We make small problems appear bigger and insurmountable, and small decisions become life and death decisions. We focus so much on the problem and our ability to solve it to the point we cannot even remember what caused the problem. The reaction triggers panic, which is what our brain will remember to associate similar situations with, so the next time we are in a similar situation, our brain responds by sending our body messages that induce similar panic every time. By meditating, we are learning to take control of our thoughts, to disassociate ourselves briefly with your thoughts so that we can better analyze them later instead of being consumed with the thoughts. Your brain now no longer registers the panicked response; instead, it registers the calm, relaxed response so the next time you are faced with a stressful situation, your brain sends the message to your body to relax and calm down.

Meditation teaches you to calm your mind and slow down your racing thoughts, and to tune in to more positive reinforcement, which in turn helps improve your cognitive and learning skills. As you continue to practice meditation, you will start to notice that you are able to focus better and rein in irrational thoughts. If you master meditation, you will be able to notice when your mind wanders off during class or work meetings and be able to rein your thoughts back to the appropriate thing you are supposed to be focusing on.

Meditation can help people suffering from anxiety attacks learn how to let go of control, especially in certain situations where they are surrounded by circumstances beyond their control that trigger their anxiety. For example, as you are preparing to leave your home for the office, you receive a phone call from a friend telling you that your company is going to be laying off staff. The phone call disrupts your routine and you leave the house five minutes later than you planned, and as you reach the bus stop you find that the bus was early today and that the next bus is going to be coming in the next thirty minutes, which means you will be late to work.

Your natural response is to panic. You have just heard that your company is laying off people, you wonder if you are now one of them and you will not have a job, which will make you unable to pay rent, which will make your landlord evict you, and then you will have to live in the streets. Your thoughts have made you blow the situation out of proportion, which induces more panic that makes you unable to handle the situation. If you are someone who regularly practices meditation, you will realize after you miss the bus that you have other options. You can call someone and see if they will be able to drop you, or you can call your boss and explain that you are running a few minutes late. You realize that you can remain calm even if you are stuck in a bad situation.

To start meditating, look for a quiet place where you will not be disturbed or easily distracted. Focus all your thoughts on one object or word; you can also choose just a sound such as "mmh" and gently repeat that word or sound for around twenty minutes. Some people find it beneficial to use their breathing pattern as something they can focus on for the stipulated twenty minutes. Basically, in meditation, what you are doing is quieting your mind and allowing it to focus on one thing at a time. This process of meditation can help you learn how to process your thoughts when you panic. For instance, when you are called to give a presentation at school or at the office and your thoughts tell you that people will laugh at what you will say, or that you are not adequately prepared, then you reinforce those thoughts by seeing yourself fainting or forgetting everything. Notice that by this time, your thoughts and feeling are out of sync with the reality — nobody has heard your presentation so how can they think it's stupid? To gain control of our emotions, we need to learn to distract ourselves from negative thoughts.

Chapter 2.   Anxiety Explained

Anxiety can be difficult for people to recognize when they are first experiencing it. Most people, in fact, might mistake it for a physical health problem due to the symptoms that accompany it. At its core, anxiety is a response to stress. It makes people feel scared or worried about certain situations for a variety of reasons. Some people might be worried that others will judge them for how they act or speak, others might be afraid that some harm will come to them if they put themselves in a certain situation. These feelings are not all abnormal, however. Some common anxiety-inducing situations include a child's first day of school, an initial job interview, or someone's wedding day. These experiences can all cause anxiety due to the uncertainty of the situation and might cause a person to start thinking about worst-case scenarios.

All of these feelings are part of anxiety because it was the evolutionary way of keeping people safe when their environment was inherently dangerous. The heightening of senses and increased heart rate prepares the body to run or fight if presented with danger, which could have meant life or death in prehistoric times. Today, however, people are not faced with imminent death on a daily basis, but their brain might not know how to adjust itself to the safety of modern life. It can still trigger anxious feelings if it is threatened to encourage a person to flee the situation, even if the reasons are not rational.

Some people experience anxiety to an extreme degree and can feel like their negative thoughts are unrelenting. For someone with this level of anxiety, quieting their mind and finding any kind of relief can be especially difficult and might even seem impossible. If a person suffers from anxiety of this intensity for an extended period of time, they might fit the criteria for an anxiety disorder. Typically, to qualify for a disorder diagnosis, a person has to experience symptoms for longer than six months or the symptoms need to be interfering with their daily life.

There are a variety of anxiety disorders that are all defined by how the anxiety affects someone or what causes anxious feelings. Each person is different, even though they might experience similar symptoms of anxiety, and the way their anxiety affects them can make a big difference in a diagnosis. Among these disorders is a plethora of negative side effects caused by the increased levels of stress and constant negative thoughts. Some people have trouble sleeping at night, have trouble concentrating during the day, find interacting with others especially difficult, or are too afraid to leave their own homes.

Some common anxiety disorders include panic disorder, phobias, social anxiety disorder, and separation anxiety. Obsessive-compulsive disorder is no longer considered an anxiety disorder, but people diagnosed with it often experience severe anxiety as one of their symptoms. Each of these common disorders associate anxiety with a particular object, situation, or action. These disorders can severely affect a person's life by making them unable to perform daily tasks or prevent them from enjoying their hobbies. For example, someone with agoraphobia—fear of crowds—may become so debilitated by fear that they refuse to leave their home.

The symptoms of anxiety are not necessarily universal and can vary greatly from person to person. Sometimes the reason a person has anxiety can determine their symptoms, as well. For example, someone who has anxiety because they think they are in danger might feel a pounding heart because their body wants to escape. Another person, however, who is dreading a social interaction, might experience an upset stomach due to the increased stress. Symptoms can range from gastrointestinal issues to cardiovascular discomfort, headaches, and in extreme cases even vomiting if stress builds up enough with the anxiety.

At the onset of symptoms, some people may suddenly feel like they are no longer in control of their body. This can often increase feelings of anxiety because they may not feel like the dread or physical symptoms will ever subside. Sometimes this out of control feeling can even lead to panic attacks. Other startling symptoms can include nightmares or constantly recalling painful thoughts or memories. These can also contribute to increased stress and anxiety because a person might feel like they cannot escape their own negative thoughts or what might seem to be an inevitably painful outcome of an event.

In people with generalized anxiety, it is more common to worry about things because of a past experience. For example, if a child's parent forgot them in a grocery store for an extended time, that child might then develop a fear of grocery stores and feel unsafe when they go to one. This could potentially carry on into adulthood, even if the person doesn't remember the event that instigated their anxiety. Common symptoms of this type of anxiety usually present themselves when a person is in a certain situation or sometimes if they merely consider putting themselves in the trigger situation. These people often experience a racing heart, shortness of breath or rapid breathing, restlessness, trouble focusing, and a slew of other symptoms.

Anxiety can even affect a person's stomach function, causing gas, constipation, or diarrhea when it flares up. This can also contribute to more severe anxiety in a person because they may become fixated on their stomach problems and convinced that if they are in a social situation, they might have a problem they cannot get away to handle. Some people can experience this discomfort even at the thought of doing something that gives them anxiety. This is why it can be particularly difficult for people to overcome their anxiety. If even the thought of doing something makes them feel physically ill, it can be difficult to convince themselves that actually doing it won't be painful.

When people experience these intense physical symptoms in relation to their anxiety, it can often cause them to start avoiding things, situations, or people that they believe will trigger their negative feelings. Although this might seem like an effective coping mechanism to those with anxiety, it can actually severely limit their lives by making them unable to participate in normal everyday tasks. On top of wanting to avoid these situations, anxiety can make a person feel too weak or fatigued to engage in social activities. This further cements their desire to withdraw and stay confined to their safe space instead of facing and managing their anxiety.

Recognizing Stress: How to Calm your Body

Did you know that one-third of the United States population reported to experiencing extreme levels of stress? These statistics were obtained from a 2007 poll of the American Psychological Association. This was more than a decade ago. Now imagine what the percentage will be now with all that's going on in the free world. Stress has the tendency of making people feel overwhelmed with the goings-on around them. According to that poll, about one in every five persons reported that they experience high levels of stress not less than fifteen days in every month. Although it has been proved that low levels of stress do not pose any immediate threat to your health, but escalated and poorly managed stress can produce life threatening conditions. Your ability to recognize high stress levels and the stressors will help you know the exact ways to act promptly in the healthiest ways that will help you change unhealthy behaviors, thereby regaining and maintaining control over your health. And for you to achieve this, there are situations you must pay attention to. Paying attention to those situations will help you understand your stress pattern, the stressors, and how you can avoid future occurrences.

You should be aware of your stress pattern

Being that everyone experiences stress differently and on different occasions, understanding how your stress occurs, what your stressors are and how you get to understand that you are stressed will go a long way in helping you maintaining calmness during and after a stressful episode. Also, your ability to understand how you react to stressful situations is also important. This concerns your thoughts and behavior and how they align with or react to your stressors and stress. When you understand this, you will be able to point out the difference in your behavior during the times you are stressed and the times when you're not.

You should identify the sources of your stress

Identifying the sources of your stress also means shooting the dart on your stressors. To do this effectively, you have to be more attentive to the moments before a stressful situation. The reason for the extra attention is for you to identify the particular events or situations that trigger stress feelings. Being able to do this will go a long way in helping you plan your life or change your lifestyle. For instance, if you discover that the relationship that exists between you and your family members, or between you and your employer or a colleague at work, or the relationship that exists between you and a neighbor is your stressor, what you do after this discovery will determine whether you deal with stress and maintain good health, or whether these stressors will continue to haunt you at the expense of your health.

There is also the possibility of your stressor arising from financial predicaments or decisions. It could be from much workload or the lack of a job. It could be from the consequences of a bad decision. Whatever you identify as your stressor, you should know that taking steps to avoid or discontinue their activities in your life will help you calm your body.

You should be aware of your own stress signal

Not everybody experiences the same signs and symptoms of stress. Whereas some people's manifestation might show minor signs like increased heartbeat and profuse sweating, some other people's manifestation might be observed through major signs like heightened alertness, extreme anxiety or panic attacks. You might realize that when you are stressed, you usually have a hard time articulating your thoughts well or failing at general body coordination. But this might be for you and your way of showing signs of stress. For someone else, it may be inability to concentrate, inability or difficulty in making sound decision, anger and rage mostly over minor issues, headaches and migraine, muscle tension or excessive tiredness. Amongst all these signals and the ones not mentioned, knowing what your signal is will help you identify stressful moments. This way, you will be better informed on how to handle them and calm your body at the same time.

You should identify how you deal with stress

How do you deal with stress? Do you calm yourself by engaging in healthy activities or do you worsen your situation by practicing unhealthy behaviors like drinking, smoking, taking hard drugs, engaging in sexual adventures, denying yourself food, binge eating, or all of them? If the way you deal with stress is by engaging in the above bad habits, then you should know that the relief you think you get from them is just temporal. Such activities will not help you calm your body, and if you do them as often as you're stressed, you will develop an addiction to them. You already know how burdensome and unhealthy addictive behaviors are; you should have the presence of mind to avoid them. There are healthy ways to deal with stress and these ways will be explained in as the book progresses.

Being able to identify these behaviors as coping mechanism will help you understand how your body reacts to stress and what you should do to restore calmness to your body.

Identifying healthy ways to manage your stress

There are tons of stress-reducing and controlling activities you can engage in if you want to effectively manage your stress and emerge from it healthier and renewed. You should consider all the stress management tips available such as meditation, exercising, therapies (with include talking to a professional psychologist, attending interactive group sessions, taking up cognitive behavior therapy sessions, talking to families, friends and other people you feel safe to talk to, and seeing a life coach), and engaging in activities that calms your mind.

Your ability to identify healthy ways to deal with stress should also include avoiding every form of unhealthy behavior. You should keep it in mind that unhealthy behaviors develop gradually, and when they are learned you find them a tad bit difficult to unlearn. Hence, in learning new and rewarding behaviors and habits and dropping negative ones, you should follow a gradual process. If you try to drop them all at once, it might prove much of a task for you. Remember that the target is to enter and remain in a state of calmness.

Myths about Anxiety and Panic Attacks

"You Are Weak"

I still recall the pep talks other people gave me when I suffered from debilitating anxiety. "Just get over it. It's all in your head" or even "Man up!" Some would even ask, "Why do you get so worked up over nothing?"

Other phrases I was offered were: "You're just working too hard. You need to relax" and "You're too stressed. Why don't you try some yoga?"

They had no idea what I was going through. They simply didn't get it.

Friends, family, and my girlfriend at the time didn't understand. If I had severely cut my finger while practicing chainsaw juggling, then they would have at least seen something was wrong with me. But my brokenness was hidden. They often thought I was imagining it. They presumed I was weak, and some didn't even hide their opinion.

Imagine a soldier running through a terrorist-infested city somewhere in the desert. He's alone and should wait for reinforcements, but he doesn't, being the brave man he is. He keeps going.

As beads of sweat run down his face, he hears gunfire coming from the left and right. He quickly looks up but can't see the shooters. He can hear the bullets fly right by him, and he feels the subtle air stream they create as they swirl past his head, barely missing him. The soldier decides to be strong and to keep going, even though he's terrified and panicking in every way possible.

The question is: is this soldier weak?

Of course not!

This is a picture of what truly debilitating anxiety or panic attacks feel like. You're under fire, but you have no idea where the danger is coming from. Doing whatever it is you fear, even if it's something simple like boarding an airplane or giving a speech, is as brave as the soldier running through a war zone. It launches the same defense systems in your body.

You are not weak. You are, in fact, very brave. What can be a walk in the park to them can feel like going to a war zone for you. Even my therapists and psychiatrists didn't really understand. They wanted to help, and I respect them for that. They cared, but to me, it always felt as if they thought I was exaggerating, especially with the pointless techniques they kept suggesting. I got the feeling that they just didn't get it. Even though they meant well.

The longer your anxiety sticks around, the more other people will start to get fed up with your excuses to avoid doing that what you fear. Some might even take it personally and believe you simply don't like them.

This can happen to anyone, by the way. I've helped people from all walks of life from the big-time CEO to the intern or student whose life is just getting started. I've helped people of all ages, from the 14-year-old whose mother had contacted me to the 84-year-old man who had been living with his anxiety for over fifty years.

Some of my clients are psychiatrists or medical doctors. I've even had an airline pilot once who was afraid of flying. Yes, it happened. And I'm sure you can imagine how ashamed he was to admit this to anyone. "Welcome aboard. This is your captain speaking. Sit back and relax and enjoy the flight. And if there's anyone with a fear of flying, don't worry, you're not alone. I'm scared to death as well!"

You are not weak! Anxiety can strike anyone at any time. When the anxiety system starts to run afoul, it will take over your life... until you stop it. And that's why I wrote this book. I want to help you deactivate your panic attacks and eliminate your unnecessary anxiety.

The Power Is Already Within You

You won't need a miracle or a wish-granting genie to overcome your anxiety. The power is already within you.

You won't need to change your genes or hire the DeLorean from the movie Back to the Future to go back in time and fix something that went wrong. Even though the problem started in the past, we cannot and need not change the past. Talking about the past does not fix panic attacks or anxiety. There are things you are doing now, each and every day, that maintain the anxiety. Those are the true and current causes that you'll have to remove.

Four years ago, a man from France followed my course. He was 84 when he found my website and ordered the French version of my audio course. He had been suffering from severe panic attacks since the age of 29, that's fifty-five years! Six months after starting the audio course, he e-mailed me explaining he had overcome his panic attacks. About a year after, his wife thanked me for giving them the best time of their lives.

Fifty-five years of panic attacks... can you imagine? I didn't prescribe any pills (I'm not a doctor); I didn't use any voodoo or magic spells, and I didn't put on my angel wings since I don't have any. The power was already within him, and it had been all that time. I simply showed him how to use it, just as I'll show you now.

How to Feel Totally Calm During Moments of Intense Anxiety

I bet this title sounds like a dream, doesn't it? What if I were to present you with a formula that would help you to be totally calm, cool, and collected during moments of intense anxiety? Would that be something you're interested in?

I bet you are. And this may be the very reason why your anxiety is so persistent!

That's because it is the wrong approach.

When you suffer from unwanted anxiety, the goal is never to feel calm. The goal is not to take your anxiety away. Please allow me to explain since I understand this may sound very odd.

The more you try to make the anxiety go away, the more you try to stay calm, the more you try to make your symptoms disappear, the worse it will get!

And I guess I don't even have to prove this. You have already experienced it plenty of times or you wouldn't be reading this book.

The more the anxiety upsets you, the more power you give it.

Trying to avoid anxiety or attempting to make it vanish is a form of resistance, and the anxiety you're feeling already represents resistance to something that's happening or that you were thinking about. That's what launched the anxiety in the first place. Hence, the more resistance you add, the more you forcefully try to be calm, the more nervous you will get.

It's the equivalent of pouring gasoline on a fire in an effort to extinguish the flames. Or trying to fall asleep by frantically hoping you will fall asleep soon. How well does that work?

When you are anxious, your nervous system is already freaking out. We shouldn't increase the pressure.

This was one of the many mistakes I was making in the past. I'll explain more later, but I wanted to set this straight from the start.

Goal number one is not to take your anxiety away; that happens at a later stage. First, we'll need to work on your intolerance to anxiety because that's the true root cause of what you're currently dealing with.

For now, remember that one of the most calming emotions you can give yourself is realizing that it is OK to let go of control, to let things flow and just see what happens. Even when what you are experiencing is as pleasant as an unwanted hug from a stranger who forgot to shower or apply deodorant for the last seven months.

The more you fight anxiety, the worse it will get. The more you let go, the faster it will pass.

Easier said than done, of course. Let's try to make it as easy as possible.

Why Are We So Anxious?

How did this happen? You're smart. You're doing the best you can, trying to make something of your life. And then, all of a sudden, anxiety tries to ruin it all.

It often starts out small. One event, one little thing where it rears its ugly head and shows you what it's capable of.

Then, like any sane human being would, you think, "Well, I hope that doesn't happen again" and the fear of the fear is born.

This attitude then sets a chain of events in motion where, through a slow process, anxiety will try to dominate your life more and more. Oftentimes there will be things you used to do without blinking that now make you lie awake at night weeks before the event. At that point, anxiety starts to overshadow everything.

If you suffer from anxiety, you are not alone. According to the Anxiety and Depression Association of America (ADAA) and the National Institute of Mental Health, an estimated 18% of the population suffers from anxiety-related issues, with or without panic attacks.

Many people who have contacted me over the years believed their anxiety was unique, that there was something wrong with them. I was no different. It honestly even took me a long time finding out that it was anxiety disturbing me, for at first, I simply believed there was a major, overlooked issue within my body.

Whatever it is you fear, whatever your thoughts, you are not alone. You are not broken, and there is nothing wrong with the chemical substances in your brain. I've heard it all during the more than a decade of helping people with anxiety and panic attacks.

I've been there too. I thought I was the only one with those weird thoughts and reactions I used to suffer from. You are not abnormal. You're just being flooded by negative thoughts that, for now, you choose to follow and put emphasis upon.

The reason why you may feel unique is because you can't see anxiety, let alone anxious thoughts. I have some famous celebrities on my client list and, upon looking at their public lives, you cannot imagine the anxieties they face. They seem (and are) very strong, yet they too are burdened with unwanted anxiety, unwanted thoughts, and feelings they'd rather avoid. I once had a famous violin player as a client who had panic attacks during her concerts. The audience and even I couldn't see it. Yet, she was in the midst of dealing with a full-blown panic attack.

Everyone has anxiety to some extent, a lot of people have panic attacks, and some people you've been in the same room with have had a panic attack while you were present. They were simply really good at hiding it, just as you undoubtedly are or at least try to be. Not everyone feels comfortable openly talking about them. We'll talk about this sense of shame later in the book, because that's an important part of the problem too.

Relaxation Techniques for Anxiety

Relaxation is an incredibly effective way of dealing with anxiety, and it applies to all groups of people. It allows the body to activate its natural response to combat stressors. Relaxation comes in many forms and depends on what works best for you. Some of the relaxation techniques that have been proven to beat back anxiety are:

·   Relaxation exercises such as muscle relaxation and deep breathing

·   Meditation

·   Visualization

·   Physical activities like yoga

There is a common belief among many people that relaxation involves sitting idle and or doing something you enjoy, like watching a movie or sleeping. No, relaxation is a task that needs concentration and energy input. Its sole purpose is to reduce the effects of stress and anxiety. If your definition of relaxation doesn't meet this goal, then it is far from relaxation. Relaxation achieves this by putting your body to a state of deep rest and restores normalcy such as slowing the heart rate, reducing blood pressure, improve blood circulation and, most importantly, checking stress and anxiety. Activities that involve relaxation are those that touch on the most affected organs like the heart, blood vessels, and those in the breathing system. Try things like muscular exercises, meditation, yoga, and deep breathing. Most of these exercises are a form of self-treatment, so you don't need a professional to do them. However, they are quite demanding and require a lot of discipline. If you are the type that needs to be pushed, you might consider looking for a professional therapist to help you do the exercises. The word 'professional' is key because not anybody can make you do things that make you uncomfortable, especially if you're an adult. You need someone that will be hard and a little harsh on you. Also, people have diverse systems that respond differently to changes. If one or two of these exercises don't work for you, look for one that you are comfortable doing and is compatible with your system. You don't have to kill yourself trying to make a particular technique work even you can see that it is not working. Furthermore, all these techniques have been proven to lead to the same results, which is slowing down stress and anxiety. Just don't be too lazy to give a particular technique trial and error period before giving up on it entirely. Remember things take time; you need to give your body a chance to get used to these changes. You will get used to those exercises in no time, and they will become a habit.

There is a thin line between relaxation exercises and meditation exercises. The main difference being that relaxation exercises engage various parts of the physical body while meditation engages the brain. The similarity between them is that they both put the entire body and mind in a state of rest to relief affected parts and organs from stress and anxiety. Both exercises are carried out in systematic steps to the end. Skipping one step will likely jeopardize the whole process. If you are not sure about these steps and the order in which they are done, it is advisable that you seek the help of a therapist who will take you through each step.

There are various exercises that involve relaxation, as discussed below.

Deep Breathing

This is the bedrock of all other relaxation exercises. It is the simplest yet very effective way of keeping your anxiety level in check. It communicates safety to the brain, thus easing tension, stress, and anxiety. It involves improving your breathing by cleansing and opening air cavities for normal breathing to occur. Anybody can do this without any difficulty. It doesn't matter where you do it, anywhere is a perfect place as long as the environment is conducive. Conducive means it is free from noise and particle pollution. There should also be minimal disruption from other people and things. Remember, this is a procedure with its own timeline; if you are interrupted, say in the third step, you won't resume the exercise from the third step. You will have to start all over again and make sure it goes to completion. This is the procedure:

Identify a quiet spot outdoors, say in the park, or lock yourself up in a clean, well-ventilated room. You can also sit down on a chair with your feet touching the ground or lie down with your body straight against the ground or floor. Whatever position makes you feel comfortable.

Sit up straight with your legs straight against the floor or ground, spread them apart or fold them on the knees and let the back of your feet touch. Your back should not lean on anything. Your left hand should be on your abdomen and the right on the chest. Take a deep breath through your nose for as long as you can, relax the hand on your abdomen to allow the stomach muscles to relax and accommodate more air.

Exhale through your mouth for as long as you can, lightly push your stomach in and contract the muscles to push all the air out.

Repeat this process for like five minutes non-stop. Minimize the movement of the arm on your chest. Focus only on your breathing and try to shut down your brain from all thoughts, whether positive or negative. Make sure the breathing is slow and smooth, don't try to increase the pace. Do this thrice day, each exercise should last at least five minutes, but you can go up to fifteen minutes if you like.

Progressive Muscle Relaxation

This is a two-step process of muscular contraction and relaxation involving various groups of muscles in the body. This exercise is important because it demonstrates how your body physically responds to stress and anxiety. Remember, this is a mental disorder that is not easy to detect, but if we incorporate physical aspects in detection, it will be much easier to know when we are experiencing anxiety. The exercise can be combined with deep breathing to yield maximum results. For you to carry out this exercise, you must be in your best form health-wise; no muscle spasms, no back pains or recent injuries that might put unnecessary strain on the muscles. In case you have or suspect to have any of these problems, consult your doctor before starting the exercise. Here is the procedure.

Put on some comfortable loose clothing or loosen the ones you are wearing by unbuttoning top buttons and sleeves. Remove belts and shoes.

Repeat the steps as those in deep breath, do it once or twice in this step.

Look at your feet in turn, start with one and spend some seconds looking at it. Move your toes slowly and follow their movement and other induced movements within the foot. Squeeze the muscles as tightly as you can within the foot. Make sure the muscles are tense for some ten seconds before relaxing them. Notice the change and difference between the two exercises.

Repeat this for the other foot and focus on the movement and behavior of the muscles as you squeeze them, and when you relax them.

Notice what tension does to your feet. You can do this by comparing how the foot feels when in tension and when relaxed.

Shift your attention to other groups in your body, such as the hand muscles, stomach muscles, and neck and shoulder muscles. Repeat the process for each and pay attention. Notice the kind feeling associated with tensing various groups of muscles.

Relaxation by Visualizing

This technique involves playing games with the brain by showing it what it desires. It is a very effective technique to combat anxiety because it gives you temporary peace and calmness. You can cultivate this good feeling by repeating this exercise for as many times as possible until it sticks.

If you feel like you're experiencing anxiety, find a quiet place and make yourself comfortable. You can sit or stand against something like a wall.

Close your eyes, think of your ideal space — a place you would like to be in the real world or just an imaginary one.

Imagine the life there, the feeling, smell of things there, and their sounds. Think about the people you would find in that place and how awesome they are. Let that picture stick in your mind.

Open your eyes and take a deep breath, severally. Try to feel your mind and notice if you are still experiencing anxiety.

If the anxiety tries to crawl back again, close your eyes once more and retrieve the picture of your ideal place from your mind and go back there. Experience the peace, calmness, and comfort associated with that place for as long as you can.

Repeat this process every time you feel anxious and notice if there are any changes in the completion of the exercise. Remember that the effectiveness of the procedure is determined by the amount of time you give the body to process the change. It never comes that easy, so be patient.

Relaxation through Yoga

Yoga is a workout trend that has taken the world by storm in the last ten years. It combines a series of moving and stationary poses. It also involves meditation, and this makes it an all-round relaxation technique. Apart from increasing stability, stability, and general fitness, yoga is also a powerful weapon to fight anxiety. The following different types of yoga deal with different bodily and mental problems.

Satyananda yoga- this traditional form of yoga is usually considered to be the original yoga. It is centered on meditation though it also incorporates slow poses and deep breathing. This gives it an incredible ability to combat anxiety and other psychological disorders. It is the easiest type of yoga if you are a beginner.

Hatha yoga- this type of yoga involves moderate poses and movements. After mastering all aspects of Satyananda yoga, hatha yoga is the next step to sharpen your yoga skills and improve your ability to keep anxiety at bay.

Power yoga- this is the most intense type of yoga; we can say it is a reserve of the pros. However, these intense poses gives you the ability to deal with intense stress.

Tai chi- most authors don't consider this a type of yoga, but there is a strong reason to classify it as yoga. It involves moving your body in a slow, systematic pattern and accompany it with slow but deep breathing. It is a powerful relaxation method to relieve stress and anxiety.

Like we have seen earlier, meditation is more of a psychological approach to combat anxiety. It involves freeing your mind to choose thoughts with the hope that this will serve as a counter-trigger. There are two main types of meditation.

Mindfulness Meditation

The effectiveness of this method has been put to the test by therapists, physicians, and psychologists for the last two decades. The results have been quite impressive, and it has since been used as a tool to relieve the mind from stress and anxiety. How exactly this method works is still a mystery, but it remains a powerful anxiety therapy method. Some authors have suggested that it works by confining the brain to the present, and by doing that, it shuts down traumatic memories and uncertainties of the future. This makes a lot of sense because most stresses are caused by trauma and fear of what might happen. By eliminating these two, the brain can then focus only on current events. Events that deal with reality, free of perceived threats. This is how to practice mindfulness:

Repeat all the steps as with deep breathing above. Focus on your breath alone, follow every inhalation and exhalation for as long as you can.

Monitor your mind as you focus on your breathing. Try to notice when your thoughts are about to wander and try to follow them. Notice the sounds, smells, and types of worries that your mind picks, then try to bring them back by going back to focusing on your breathing.

Allow your mind to wander once more, not anything particular, but to anything it wants. Let this wandering go on for a while then bring it back again by focusing on your breathing.

Repeat the process for about 10 minutes, twice a day or five times a week. Notice if there is any change in the level of anxiety from when you started the exercise.

Body Scan Meditation

This technique is almost similar to progressive muscle relaxation. The only difference is that it involves listening to the reaction of other parts of the body to muscular movement without judgment. This is the procedure for body scan meditation.

Lie on your back, relax your hands on your sides and keep your legs straight or crossed. Close your eyes and take a deep breath through the nose and exhale through the mouth. Follow your breathing for like five minutes.

Shift your focus to your feet, contract the muscles of the right foot, and notice the movement of the toes. Feel the effect this tension on the muscles has on different parts of the body as you tense them even tighter.

Repeat this process for the left foot and feel the tension in other regions.

Move to a different body part, say your thighs, and repeat this process. Try noticing the impact this tension has on other parts of the body. Keep moving to your knees, calf, torso, abdomen until you have scanned every part.

After you are done, sit in stillness and quietness and try to remember what you felt in different parts and organs during the exercise.

Repeat this procedure twice or thrice a day and notice the changes in your level of anxiety.

Benefits of Relaxation Techniques

All these techniques have a wide range of benefits both to the body and to the mind. Apart from the benefit of managing anxiety, relaxation techniques are helpful in various other areas as follows:

Improved breathing- techniques that involve deep breathing like meditation and yoga play an important role in opening up air pipes and facilitating the free flow of clean air in and out of the system. Even if one experiences anxiety, chances are that their breathing system will not be harmed.

Mental stability- these exercises and techniques do not only curb anxiety, but they also prevent many other psychological and mental disorders, so you are actually killing two birds with one stone. This is made possible when you keep your mind busy and divert it from the cause of anxiety. This diversion applies to other underlying conditions of the mind.

Spices up one's social life- most of these relaxation activities and techniques are done in groups such as yoga classes and Tai chi. They expose one to different kinds of people and actually make them more sociable. Once someone starts socializing with others, the chances are that they will talk about their problems and get help.

Boosts confidence- anxiety becomes worse if the affected individual considers themselves weak. As soon as these exercises start gaining momentum, you will notice a feeling of self-pride and confidence running through you. This is a hidden benefit of applying these relaxation techniques.

Engages the brain- most people would actually use their free time to worry about ambiguous threats. This will only increase their chances of developing anxiety. Participating in these relaxation exercises will engage the brain, and you won't be thinking about some imaginary threats and problems. By the time you are done with the exercise, it will be time to resume your normal duties, and this keeps your too brain busy to indulge in unhealthy thinking.

Keep in mind that not everyone responds well to anxiety exercises and relaxation techniques. The symptoms may actually worsen for some people. If you notice that these exercises are not doing you any good, go see a doctor immediately for further direction. Seeking professional help is important since you might be suffering from other hidden illnesses.

Explanation of the Reference Technique

This is a technique that attempts to divert the mind from a perceived threat or source of anxiety by shutting down most body reflexes that receive, process, and respond to these threats. It is very effective in offering self-therapy when dealing with anxiety and other psychological disorders. The reference technique follows the following steps.

Find a comfortable and quiet place, and sit down, close your eyes.

Think of things that follow a chronological order like numbers, letters of the alphabet, months, or days. Start counting from the start to the end. Start counting again but this time in the opposite direction, from the last to the first.

Focus attention on various parts of the body as you do the counting. Notice if there is some reducing tension in some groups of muscles like those in the abdomen, back, and neck. Don't stop counting as you do the listening.

Suspend all muscular activities by turning off the muscles. Don't tense or relax them; just stay still, and focus on your counting.

Release your mind to think about anything, give it the freedom to wander from one thought to another, including your worries. Don't try and stop it if it tries to think about unpleasant things. Just listen and view the pictures without being judgmental.

After allowing your mind to wander on all kinds of thoughts, now start sorting out those thoughts. Removing all negative thoughts, those that you consider unpleasant and makes you worried. Only remain with positive thoughts and statements that make you feel safe and peaceful. Reflect on these positive thoughts for like two minutes.

Open your eyes, take a deep breath, and reflect on the feeling you have just experienced before opening your eyes.

Repeat this for some two times every day and notice whether your level of anxiety is changing from the first day.

Aromatherapy Can Help, Let's use Creativity!

I will compare this unique kind of self-therapy with an expectant woman. Some ladies are known to develop strange behaviors when pregnant. One of them is cravings. You will be surprised to learn some have the weirdest cravings. My first cousin is one such woman. When she was five months pregnant, I happened to have visited her place. Everything was okay until she woke up in the dead of night, demanding petrol. Yes, you heard that, right! She was not using a generator, nor did she have a car that uses petrol. When her husband asked her what she wants petrol for, she gave a hilarious answer that left us in stitches. She just wanted a little to sniff. When we were still treating her demand as a joke, she started behaving weirdly. She looked like she was about to have a panic attack. We had to join the village witches in that ungodly hour with a jar, walking from house to house at 4 AM. We were lucky enough to find a good neighbor who braved the morning cold and siphoned for us some from his car. We gave it to my cousin to sniff, and she became alright, almost instantly.

Aromatherapy works exactly the same way. Aromatherapy is the alternative and integrative medication used in the control of stress and anxiety. The substance used in this procedure is a natural product or products, mostly from plants, to treat anxiety. This technique has been used since long ago for this purpose; it has a commendable record of effectiveness. So why not try it too? This is how the technique is applied to treat anxiety:

·   Collect different parts of plants, preferably of the species Matricaria recutita and Lavandula ssp. These plants might not be found in your local area, so you might have to buy the whole processed package.

·   Extract their oil through simple distillation. Store the oil in a clean container and make it airtight. Store the bottle in a dark space with a temperature of about -20 degrees Celsius.

·   Apply the oil to different parts of the body once a day for a period of two to three months. The method of application involves pouring some oil into your palm, rub it on the skin in any body part and spread it slowly and gently with your fingers. Massage yourself slowly for some ten minutes. You can ask someone else, preferably a therapist, to assist in the massaging.

·   Repeat this for different parts of the body every day until the two or three months are over.

·   Compared your level of anxiety at the end of the treatment and at the beginning to see if there has been any improvement.

The effectiveness of this natural technique in the treatment of anxiety has been proven by medical practitioners the world over. So, why not give it a try? Not as a last option but as a unique approach in combating anxiety. Just like my cousin, maybe you need just one touch of aromatherapy to heal your anxiety.

Chapter 3.   An   Overview   of Mindfulness

You may think that you know all the answers, but no one really does. Thus, worrying about things makes the problems larger than life, and thus they become negative and weigh your mind down. Mindfulness, on the other hand, is being aware of your surroundings, being more aware of nature, and even more aware of your own body. How does this help? It calms the mind and allows it to get away from negative thinking.

Now I know this sounds rather philosophical and impractical. But mindfulness is a real technique, which you can employ to better your thinking and also your overall life.

Although thought of as a new approach by many, Buddhist monks have been doing mindful meditation for centuries. There are those who question how you can be meditative to the point of being aware and still be mindful. They argue that the two elements "mindfulness" and "meditation" contradict each other. Actually, they couldn't be more wrong. When you meditate, your mind is working. It may be concentrating on a mantra, or focusing upon a certain object within a room or thinking about the breaths that you take. The mind doesn't close down, so why not make it more aware of what it is doing? Mindfulness does that. It means not only being aware of yourself, your actions, your reactions to other people, but also being aware of what they are saying and listening to problems rather than taking them, exaggerating them, and watching them become stresses and worries.

The problem is that when you fill your mind with worries, you have no room in your mind for positive thoughts. The worries build up and what you inevitably find is that they become even more negative. That's why there are so many people with miserable faces and so many who can't face another day. These are people who may ask for medical help for depression or who may eventually suffer heart or other health problems because the worries took over and took an eventual strain on the body. That's how powerful thought is. It can turn your life upside down. However, when you begin to live your life in a mindful way, you begin to find that you have less room for negativity and that you are able to see the good side of life. This, in turn, makes you feel healthier and happier than you have ever felt before and that's got to be worthwhile.

Have you ever wondered what you are missing in life? Well, close your eyes and then describe the person who works opposite you every day. Ask yourself what that person is wearing today. Ask yourself what's on his/her desk and what the last thing that the person said to you was. The chances are that you will get it wrong because people are not mindful of others and certainly not that mindful about the life that they are letting slip through their fingers.

Mindfulness is a state of mind, but it's also a way of life. When you see people whose lives seem more fortunate than yours, never measure this in terms of money. Look how happy they are. There are certain people who attain great happiness and who spread that toward others. There are others who are perpetually miserable and insist on sharing that with others and yet others who choose to hide behind medication or seeking medical advice because the mind seems out of control. Perhaps it is, but perhaps it's simply a question of changing routes and finding out all about the way mindfulness helps you to become less worried and more trouble-free.

There are, of course, two different kinds of personality as well to contend with. There are those who see the glass as half full, while others see it as half empty. Did you ever wonder why? Pessimism and negativity are not something that mindful people need to worry too much about. They are too busy taking the ride of their lives and enjoying every moment of it to even get into negative thoughts. You can too, but you need to know how. It's a question of retraining your mind to think in another way. Once you do, you will never look back and never regret having taken that decision. It's a true-life changer.

Putting Mindfulness to Work

Strangely enough, mindfulness is a paradox. It is the easiest thing in the world to practice, and it can also be the hardest. For instance, if I asked you to take a look at your right hand

and pay close attention to it, you would be able to do it within a second! You would be able to pick out the different tones and colors in your skin, the blemishes and the marks, the lines on your palms and their movements, the webbing between your fingers, etc., etc. You would take in every detail without difficulty and then flex your hand in and out to feel the movement as much as see it, thereby evoking more than one sensory perception.

That, in essence, is mindfulness. And it can be hard to take it. Something as simple as noticing your hand can be done easily; try to translate this practice to the basest of your feelings, like your deepest anger or sorrow. And if you move from the emotional to the physical pain, you would have to take in the way your entire body aches after a long work out or the way your head throbs after a long day at work – it is not a pleasant prospect. Mindfulness requires that we feel and experience every action, every reaction and every situation to the fullest, whether it is joy or sorrow. As human beings, it is rather natural that we would want to partake more of the former and less of the latter. What we fail to realize is that they are interconnected; you cannot have one without the other, and both are vital to the growth of the human mind.

So before we begin and get down to the nitty-gritty details on how to be more mindful, here are a few things you need to keep in mind. They are sort of a prep-stage for you, a general mindset to adopt so that you can take it slow and be successful.

Start Easy

Mindfulness is really a way of life, instead of just a few specific exercises that will change your life around. It is, like tackling diabetes, a lifestyle change that you will need to make. And these are not easy to do. Don't expect yourself to perform miracles in a matter of days; start small and take each day as it comes.

To boost your state of mindfulness, start out by paying closer attention to things. And when I say things, I don't mean just the things that surround you or your environment; I mean, pay attention to yourself in relation to these things. For instance, if something makes you happy, then take that minute to savor that happiness. Allow yourself to feel that moment in full and then let it go. That sounds very out there, doesn't it? Okay, then try something a bit more practical – when you walk into your kitchen on a hot day and drink water, feel that first, cold sip to the fullest. Feel the coldness of the water you're holding through the glass, savor the way it wets your tongue, and then slides down the length of your throat. Feel the glass itself and the cool tips of your fingers holding. In short, experience every sensory perception you can in that single sip of water.

You can see why this might be tiring to do day after day. Having to pay that much close attention to everything gets annoying after a while – the problem lies in the fact that we expect miracles in days. Start out small and take it step by step. Remember, there is no right or wrong way to do this and nobody is going to penalize you for not doing it more than a couple of hours. Make a beginning by simply paying closer attention to yourself – if you can do that, you're a champ already!

Practice any type of Mindfulness that suits you

The thing about mindfulness is that there is no right way or no wrong way to do it. It can be done anytime and anywhere. The only thing you require is the motivation to do it. Modern myths of mindfulness paint pictures of Buddhist enthusiasts sitting in a calm, peaceful setting and meditating deeply, with the soft smell of incense in the background and gentle music coloring the air. This stereotypical image will come into play later, when we are talking about mindfulness meditation – but make no mistake, mindfulness and meditation are two entirely different activities, each with their own benefits. You don't have to meditate to be mindful; it is only advised that you do both to get the full benefit of the whole idea. They go hand-in-hand, but you need to figure out what suits you the best.

The reason such a picture is painted is because of how calm it makes the person. Sitting with your back straight in a calm setting, with soft music and aromatic smells in the air soothes the mind, making it easier to blank it out and give you that inner peace. However, while it is comfortable for meditating, it isn't necessary that you find it easy to be mindful in such a setting. For instance, you may find it easier to be mindful of yourself and your surroundings better in a more familiar environment – like at a sandbox, with your son, or at a park, with your daughter. Just sit next to them when they are playing, focus on your breathing and give them your full attention – that, in itself, is mindfulness.

Make mindfulness a habit. Take it as it is meant to be – an adverb that describes any action you are performing. What are you most comfortable making a daily habit you will perform regularly? Is it walking mindfully each morning? Is it eating every bite mindfully? Is it sitting down and meditating mindfully? Tailor the exercises to suit your needs – you are different from everybody else and as an individual, you must practice mindfulness to suit you and not anyone else.

As I mentioned before, mindfulness is a lifestyle. Think of it like training a muscle. When you start exercising, you get tired quickly and you feel the burn after, say 5 push-ups. As you keep going, soon enough that 5 will become 7, and then progress to 10 and so on. Training your mind is also a similar exercise; start out small and fix something that you can be regular in. Make it a daily routine/habit and you will find that it slowly ends up being a way of life itself.

Forgive yourself

This is perhaps the biggest challenge a lot of people face in practicing mindfulness. Negative thinking and pessimism are powerful factors that inhibit the practice of mindfulness. Paradoxically, they are the very traits many practitioners of mindfulness advocate the exercise gets rid of. Self-compassion does not come easy to most of us; I'm not talking about letting yourself get away with things, like constantly making excuses for yourself when you know you're wrong. That is a different kind of self-harm; here, I am talking about gnawing away at a mistake you made that you just cannot seem to let go of.

If you suddenly realize that you have not been mindful today, then let it go – forgive yourself. If you are too busy to think about being mindful – forgive yourself. If you are unable to stick to a single routine and you feel terrible about it – let yourself accept it and let it go. When you are trying to meditate or be mindful, and your mind just won't allow you to relax and keeps wandering off – don't get frustrated, but forgive yourself.

Remember, it is a better idea to think about what you can do now, instead of worrying and upsetting yourself over what you should have done and what you didn't do. It's a good idea to examine your actions and see where you went wrong so you don't commit the same mistake again, but to constantly self-recriminate and scold yourself is not really going to change anything or make things better. Think about what to do now instead of worrying about what you could have done. That is mindfulness.

These are some of the most important ideologies to keep in mind when you start practicing mindfulness and try to make it a way of life. Most of all, it calls for a change in attitude – it sounds clichéd, I know, but it is a definite truth. It is not easy – let's see how you can make mindfulness a better, more intimate part of your life!

Mindfulness isn't easy at first, and the first exercises that are suggested are ones that will show you how far away you are from being mindful. Lie down on a bed in a darkened room and close your eyes. See how long you can last at closing your eyes and thinking of nothing at all. The chances are that you won't last as long as you may think you can, because your mind is accustomed to busying itself with whatever the worries of the day are. Try this several times because it gives you an idea of how much work you need to put into your mindfulness practice. If you are anything like me, you will take a little bit of time to get used to blank out the mind.

If you practice this for a few minutes every day, you may find that you are more able to do it the more you practice. However, that isn't what mindfulness is about. That's just to calm you and make you more aware that your brain needs a rest.

Greater Understanding

Buddhist philosophy views mindfulness as being the path one needs to take in order to understand the truth about the universe. There's a lot of moving parts to that statement, so let's break it down a bit. First is the detail regarding mindfulness being a path. You see, practicing mindfulness isn't just about doing a few exercises, as I've mentioned before, it's about living a certain way.

As you live mindfully, you'll learn more about yourself and how your mind reacts. When you keep progressing along this path, at some point, you'll realize that you can observe the same delusions you operate under in others around you. You'll begin to detect that point in time where your brain or the other person's brain chooses to react to the sensory stimulus they receive.

You'll notice that between the moment when something happens to you and the moment when you decide to react to it, there exists a gap. The gap is the most peaceful state of being and true presence is found here. It will be a fleeting thing and you will chase it. Once you chase it enough, you'll realize that it has always been there, and you need to allow it to exist instead of running after an image of it.

This is just a small taste of the path that will unfold before you. Everyone experiences things differently, and this is why mindfulness isn't a path of understanding the world as much as it is all about figuring out who you are. Is there even a difference between understanding yourself and the universe? You'll find out!

This brings us to the next portion of our initial sentence, which talks about "understanding." What is understanding and what is knowledge? Often the two are confused for one another. Who is better equipped to deal with the world, a person who has excellent interpersonal skills or a recluse genius mathematician? Obviously, it's the former. But who's understands things better?

Who has a better grasp of reality? This opens another line of thought. What is reality? The journey you will undertake will bring about all sorts of questions like these. It is easy and very pleasing to our ego to sit around and pontificate about all of these things, but the fact is that all of our opinions about these things are worth as much as a piece of garbage in the overall scheme of things.

Doing and practicing is what counts when it comes to mindfulness and without practice, you cannot hope to acquire any knowledge. The true nature of knowledge is thus the journey itself and not the destination. Along the way, as you observe what triggers you, you'll gain a deeper insight into what the nature of your reality is and how you have created it.

Reality is created by your intention. Intention is a nebulous thing and cannot be described with any great accuracy. Intention can be best thought of as the spirit with which you live your life. Ancient Buddhism opines that by fixing the right intention, a person's journey in life becomes that much easier. What is the right intention? Briefly, it is to practice right actions and right thoughts.

What are right actions and thoughts? Well, at this point we'd be going deep into Buddhist philosophy, and that is not the point of this book. The aim is to apply mindfulness to achieve improvements in your life, namely by reducing the amount of stress you experience. So, let's just say that your actions and intentions need to be aligned on achieving a more harmonious view with the world.

This means you need to align yourself with the reality that is around you. The more your reality conflicts with what is around you, universal reality, so to speak, the greater the stress and disconnect you will experience. You expect things to go left, but the world goes right. You undertake stress.

You think you're qualified for the job, but your boss doesn't and promotes someone else instead. Stress. The world is loaded with all kinds of stress triggers for us and the mistake we make is that we try to change the world. If a loved one behaves a certain way, that annoys us, what is our typical reaction? Well, if you're like most people, you probably tell them to cut it out. You try to get them to stop.

Mindfulness will get you to realize that you cannot control things that are outside of you. The more you try to control them, the more out of sync with reality you become, and the more the suffering you heap on yourself. In this context, suffering can be thought of as being stressed.

Think back to what happens when you keep telling your loved one to change their behavior. One day they simply refuse, and this results in a dramatic fight. Good luck not getting stressed out from that! True wisdom recognizes that change only comes from within since this is the only aspect of your life you fully control. Everything else is out of your hands, and you have no business worrying about or trying to control any of that.

Progression

So, your intention is fixed in trying to align yourself to the world and to reduce the disconnect between inside and outside. What happens now? Well, once your intention changes, you begin expressing this with your thoughts and words. These are what create your reality and are how people form impressions of you.

Really what's happening is that your intention is what creates your environment. The environment we surround ourselves with is extremely important. Research has shown that we mimic the actions and behavior of the people closest to us (ANTONOPOULOS, 2016). Everything from money, success and behavior is molded by your environment, whether when you were a child or an adult.

A lot of people try to change the outside world, again, by trying to force their worldview on their environment, that is, the people around them. Some even succeed for a while but this is the wrong way to go about things. Trying to control the thoughts and the will of others is a futile task, and when it does blow up, it's pretty spectacular. Think back to how any dictator or despot has received their comeuppance.

Here, again, we see that the thing to do is to change your intention and allow this to change your environment. The actions you need to take are very little in this case. After all, you only need to seek to align yourself with where you want to be in your life. One of the biggest causes of stress is the fact that people are in one place and they want to be in another.

They might say their intention is to be elsewhere, but intention is betrayed by action. If a person continues to behave in the old manner or doesn't seem to be making any effort with regards to changing their situation, you can safely assume their intention is exactly where they are right now.

What you think and say is what creates actions and how you act is how you'll behave. Your behavior is the sum of everything you want and currently believe. There is usually a disconnect when it comes to our beliefs and our intention. This isn't as big of a deal as it sounds. I mean to say that if you're in one place and want to get to another, it is obvious you're going to have to learn new things to get there.

Your belief system is shaped by your environment and thus, if you set your intention right, the environment you need will be created by you, and this will have an effect on your beliefs. Your beliefs, in turn, will further shape your environment and thus the feedback loop goes on and on.

It is in your interest to create a virtuous feedback loop instead of a vicious one, as you can imagine. Your behavior will eventually come to define who you are in the eyes of the world. The sum of your behavior in various situations is what is called character. Character is what draws people and positive situations into your life and is what people ultimately see when they look at one another.

It is easy to adopt someone's character when looking to model a successful outcome, but the fact is that you need to dig deeper and figure out what their intention is. Intention is what guides everything and is the root of your existence. Fix your intention to be mindful and present, and you'll create an environment that supports this, bit by bit.

Thought Patterns

Mindfulness will illuminate your thought patterns, as I've mentioned. By observing your mind, you'll be assuming the role of the impartial observer, not judging or questioning anything, but just observing. It sounds easy to do but the reality is a lot different. After all, you're the one you're observing, and it is hard to do this without making things personal.

If you're careening towards disaster, should you remain impersonal? No one can. The issue is that almost everything can seem like a disaster, and the process of figuring out what is a big deal and what isn't is a lot like having a bandage ripped off on an unhealed wound. It hurts.

Mindfulness isn't a passive process. It requires you to sit there and take stock of things and remain steadfast on your path. If anything, it is the most active process out there because this is how you engage in life and create a reality for yourself. There are two ways of practicing mindfulness, formal and informal.

The formal method is what monks do, which is to say that they dedicate their lives to the practice and spend long stretches of the day in meditation. Every action of theirs is informed by spiritual prescription. The informal method is to bring mindfulness to everyday actions. For example, if you're eating, becoming mindful of what you're eating and of being fully present without distraction is practicing informal mindfulness.

Personally, I find a mixture of both is the best way forward. This establishes a mindset of continuous practice and improvement. Set aside some time every day to conduct a formal practice but also keep practicing as you go about your day to the best of your abilities. Remember, if you set your intention to be mindful, you will create an environment that will encourage you to practice mindfulness.

Let's look at an example of mindful practice. Since I've mentioned eating something, we might as well begin with this. Let's say you're eating almonds and want to be more mindful of it. Pick up a single almond and begin:

1. The aim is to explore the almond with all of your senses. This is what it means to be aware of something. Set your intention as such. Act as if you've never seen it before (and you probably never truly have).
2. Run your fingers over the ridges and feel how coarse it is. Does the coarseness vary depending on the region of the almond? How do the edges feel? Do they pierce your fingers?
3. What is the shape of the solitary nut like? Keep running your fingers to understand it and feel the texture. It feels rough for sure. What about the temperature of the skin? Is it hot, cold, room temperature? As you press onto the almond, can you feel your pulse in your fingertips?
4. How does it feel in the palm of your hand? It feels small, doesn't it? Roll it around a little between your fingers and notice how different fingers react to it. As you switch fingers, can you feel the new sense of touch

running from your fingers to the inside your body via your nerves?

5. Now, smell it. Does it have a smell at all? What does it remind you of, if it does?

6. Think about wanting to eat the almond. Notice how the minute you think about it, your arm automatically moves and brings it closer to your mouth. Now, open your mouth and place it on your tongue without chewing it.

7. Roll it around inside and notice how your mouth becomes wet with saliva. This happens automatically and you didn't have to do anything to generate it. You didn't even think about it. Notice how your body is like a machine that just does things on autopilot.

8. As you're rolling it inside your mouth, think back to the thoughts that have been running through your head since the first step. What have they been? What words have they contained? Notice your reactions to those words. Don't judge, just notice and let them go. Once this is done, get back to your almond.

9. Bite it and begin to chew it. The texture feels a lot different. Notice the sound that is generated when you chew. What does your tongue feel like when the almond's insides hit your taste buds?

10. Swallow the almond and feel it pass down your throat. Notice any other internal sensations as this happens.

This exercise is just a taste of what mindfulness is all about. I'd like to note that you don't need to consciously think in this manner each and every time you do these things. Once you set your intention to be mindful, your body will follow, and you will begin to notice these things all by yourself.

As you do this, notice the number of things that are going on within you and around you. Do you realize how much of your world you simply take for granted? Think of all the things happening within your body right now. That solitary almond is contributing to this machine that is in your possession. How cool is that!

You see, this is what mindfulness does. It awakens you to things you cannot see with your eyes. Now that you've got a taste of mindfulness, let's move forward and establish a base for your mindfulness practice.

Chapter 4.   How to Deal with Stress

Over the years, I have come to believe that most people on this planet live their lives in fear of death, whether or not they truly love, and forbid their ability to live a full and beautiful life.

The reason the majority sleep in fear of death is because they do not agree or believe that they're truly loved or appreciated, or don't know their worth.

When people are truly loved, once they acknowledge their intrinsic value, value and importance, they're likely to require care of themselves and their environment. They experience fewer health problems, feel less emotionally and emotionally altered, and ultimately less anxious, afraid and angry.

Think about it: If you really loved yourself and knew what you were worth, could you not do all you could to nourish your body, mind and soul? If you feed yourself so much that you feel valued and overlooked, you won't be happy, and if someone else doesn't care or even insults you, they will offend you.

Of course you want!

You have the power to be really happy, which ability resides in your body.

You have an outsized body made from billions of cells, some strong and a few weak. Regardless of what their strength is, these cells help one another, protect one another from harm and align with one another to offer them an opportunity to measure legendary on this earth.

When these cells are not properly nourished, cared for, or supported, they cannot fully support him for life and shine, for happiness and success.

The beauty of your body is that it always lets you know when you need it, when you want to help or when it changes. Symptoms come in the form of feelings such as hunger or fatigue, cough, discomfort, or negative emotions or thoughts. These symptoms tell you when you are in stress or when you are safe, out of balance or in balance, restless or in a state of peace and love. The food you eat, the people you spend time with, the movements you make, the thoughts you hold, or the words you say have a positive or negative impact on each of your cells. In turn, these cells tell you whether your actions will help you progress or dive.

If you pay attention, you love yourself, you really want to be happy, you listen to your body's signals and defend the behaviors and actions that make you dive, and only help those who help you progress. They defend you.

You have a choice. You have the choice every day and every moment of your life whether you want to nourish or hurt your body and body. The less hurt you are, the less the world can hurt you.

You can see your life by appreciating experiences that help you discover your true self, living your life to the best of your being or expressing regret over not having enough. See yourself. That you feel your life as a victim of your own circumstances.

You have the choice of believing within the greatness of your being that it can't be undermined by another, otherwise you can believe that your existence is useless, which you'll be great as long as you're known or valued by the opposite.

If you're proud of your choice, all you've got to try to is start listening to your body's signals.

Understanding Stress

Your body speaks to you in stress. Stress is that the reason we produce, innovate, run marathons and advertise. This is, often, how we get out of bed within the morning and have an incentive to place food on the table.

When something within us wants to vary, it drives us to try it. The tendency to change is due to stress. Do you feel tired? Pressure. Are you hungry? Pressure. Low blood pressure? Stress again.

Stress is not necessarily bad. You need it to help you live, adapt and survive. It motivates us to climb mountains or innovate and find new ways to be easier or reach faster.

Stress is defined as any problem with balance (also known as homeostasis). The challenges can range from simple climate change to global news, fatal deadlines, pollution, colds, changes in blood pressure, hunger, fatigue, inflammation, lack of sleep, eating processed foods or emotional stress.

Stress can manifest itself as a challenge that endangers real life or hidden stressors, such as worrying action, feeling deficient, or a defective immune system that cannot respond to strong antibodies.

For the brain, anything that tackles the body's homeostasis is eligible for stress, and it doesn't matter if it's physical, mental, emotional, real or imaginary. As long as the brain understands that its balance is being challenged, stress is considered, and in doing so, a physiological response to stress is always mounted to solve the problem, so that it can adapt and stay alive.

The Stress Response

There are several quality reasons for a stress response or a physiological response to stress. It lifts one from bed in the morning, tells the immune system to fight off infections, the blood vessels to maintain blood pressure, and your body to move during discomfort and the sensory system to alert for hunger, cold or tiredness. Without a response to stress, you will actually be dead because it will heal wounds, survive injuries, meet nutritional needs and escape when a lion chases you.

Walter Kanon, a Harvard physiologist, preferred the term " fight or flight" in the 1930s to describe our innate defense response to threat or danger. He believed that this defense would ultimately guarantee survival. When we are in danger or in danger, we move into the bloodstream due to the release of stress hormones such as adrenaline and cortisol, which causes our senses to become too alert and excited. Our students tense to dilute and our muscles to prepare for battle or flight.

The liver releases sugar stored in the bloodstream to nourish your body, while the lungs work faster, increasing your breathing speed and making your breathing more superficial than oxygen consumption. The heart pumps harder and faster, blood pressure increases and the immune system is stimulated to mount an inflammatory response to protect it from scars or possible infections.

It is a great physiological response to be chased after by a tiger, and in the short term it will often cause physical, emotional or psychological distress of one kind or another to serve you. For example, if your blood sugar level drops, the stress response will trigger a series of physiological changes that will make you feel hungry, irritable or tired. This discomfort or negative feeling forces him to eat something to eliminate hunger or discomfort so he can regain his balance or comfort. Eating food can relieve stress so that it no longer has to be a stress response. The stress response itself turns off and allows your system to resume its stable state.

This is good news when dealing with stress and responding to stress. The bad news is that your brain can't tell the difference between stress and the other.

He cannot differentiate between running for his life and delaying his work because they both pose a threat to his livelihood somewhere in his brain. For this reason, too much stress is often activated, and in most cases, because of constant worry, it never disappears because the stress never goes away.

Perception Is Key

At this time, you may think that because you are always stressed, you are condemned, meaning that your response to stress is always active, so you are either angry or ill. Don't despair. She has the ability to solve the problem by learning how to change her perceptions of her life and her life.

The key to keeping a stress response under control is understanding. If your brain realizes that a particular situation is manageable, it triggers a stress response long enough to trigger the necessary actions, such as an athlete motivated to compete and win a race. In fact, this is what you want with a positive outlook. Positive understanding is directly related to homeland security or confidence in the success or ability to manage a particular effort or challenge. In contrast, negative perceptions are associated with low self-esteem and belief in the probability of a positive outcome.

For example, you can apologize for choosing a school for your child. You abuse this problem day and night until you feel that your life is out of control. Your anxiety stimulates the stress response, it increases your heart rate and blood pressure, the inflammation flows through your body, your memory increases your sense of blur and your cravings for comfort food or alcohol. You feel tired, in pain and overwhelmed with the desires of your life. You just don't think you can do more. Then, the child, spouse, boss, or person who fills the vacuum cleaner acts cruelly or excessively and your temper is used by you and others. The shame you experience makes you feel worse, the stress response intensifies and the cycle goes on.

Now, if you can change your mindset to believe that whatever choice you make is good, the scenario will be very different.

For example, you are very confident about your ability to make decisions, and you also believe that there is no wrong choice as each option provides opportunities for growth and learning. You know that no matter what school you send your child to, it will be great or you will find ways to make it work. She has an attitude similar to most of her life's desires, because she knows who to provide and help when needed. In this case, do you think you will explode when it is said that a boy, a wife, a boss, or someone who is filling in the papers is being ruthless? Probably not. Why? … perception.

When you consider stress to be controllable, you control the response to stress and its reactions. Understanding is really the key to resilience. The more you believe in your own ability and resources to deal with profanity, the more likely you find stress manageable, which will lead to fewer worries, more confidence, a greater sense of worth, a positive expectation, a controlled stress response. And you are stronger

If you want to benefit from a positive understanding that resources are available to access any uncertainty, you will intervene with more confidence and know that you can handle whatever is in your way. You can maintain a sense of calm, even if someone acts cruelly or disrespectfully. Your stress level is controlled. Sustainable physical health and mental and emotional clarity intact.

Consciousness Leads to A Better Understanding

If it were easy to keep positive control of stress control under control, I would not want to write this book or have a job. The important thing is that you must be aware of your stress and take care of it before controlling it. For example, you may not realize that the lack of sleep you experience as a result of striving to succeed in the workplace can cause inflammation in your body and cause more stress. You may also be aware that you keep memories that no longer serve you. These memories still define you and your understanding and lead you to success at the expense of the body. In the end, you may not realize that you are not good enough and that you have had constant stress throughout your life.

Awareness of Emotions and Memories

Emotions and emotional memory are directly correlated with physiological, positive and negative responses. Every time you experience certain emotions, your brain looks for its emotional memory bank to boost physiological and physical assumptions, beliefs, behaviors and reactions that help you cope with the past. When you face challenges that make you feel good, your brain looks for details of your memory bank to see how those challenges have been made before, what resources have been used and what the results are. It has been, and the information corresponds to your emotional memory bank. The result is a response and behavior to the challenge created by current unconscious beliefs and assumptions.

Throughout life, as one memory is reinforced over another, a belief system is formed about how you see yourself, others and the world around you, if you have enough or if you have not enough. That is not the point you have to focus on. Most people have different opinions depending on the circumstances. For example, the same person may believe that there will always be enough money because he is rich, but there is never enough love because there is no love at home.

Therefore, some of his ideas support positive expectations that his future needs will be met. Other beliefs, based on more annoying experiences, take a more negative stance and maintain negative expectations that you may never have or have enough, and you cannot rely on the world or people to help you.

This leads to circumstances that come up nowadays, where positive or negative physiological responses re produced, and subsequent beliefs and behaviors supported memory.

For example, if in the past your family always had enough money and all your needs were always met, you probably believe today that you will always get enough of what you need. Conversely, if he grew up raising food on his desk and clothes, but his parents were constantly worried about money, he would likely share some of that concern. Now, as an adult, even if you have a steady income, you may still be asking yourself, "What if I don't get it? What if I don't have enough money?" You worry about it every day and stay in a job you don't like even if you dream of doing something else, and you basically feel overwhelmed. (Do you see how this can be a source of dissatisfaction, frustration, and an easy explosion?)

Another example could be that your boss, colleague or friend disrespects you or does not follow your advice. If he was often criticized in the past, this kind of situation could make him much angrier than someone who was rarely criticized.

Whenever they criticize you, this memory is activated. When you are activated, you do what you have always done to fight: you scream, you eat, you pick, and so on. Although this behavior helps you deal with it in the short term, it does not solve anything and, in the end, it usually feels worse.

Belief Consciousness

Always remember that this is not your memory, and what has happened to you in the past is not worth it. The problem is, when you were a kid, you still didn't have much brain. In other words, when bad things happen to you, your brain interprets the situation based on limited knowledge and skills. The belief from this point of view was often distorted and incorrect. It is an irrational and false belief that drives you to respond to stress and negative behaviors.

If he had consciously focused on changing his beliefs so that a new person would eventually act in a more positive, rational, and realistic way, he would have been better able to manage his reaction and stress.

There are many techniques in the psychological and psychological worlds, including cognitive reconstruction strategies and a variety of meditation techniques.

The argument is that you can simply change your views in a negative or positive way. It is possible to separate negative emotions and perceptions from unpleasant memories and reprogram the brain with positive emotions and standards of confidence.

You can learn to understand situations differently to control them. Most importantly, you can learn to see yourself differently, love and support them by knowing that you are truly valuable. When you do, it can shake you very little.

Being in Control

When my patients decide to be self-sufficient, I found that they become healthier, more resilient, and more calm to maladaptation. Patients who are victims of living conditions, on the other hand, are less likely to face serious challenges and are more likely to be exposed to negative emotional, psychological and physical complaints.

Always remember that with the choices you make and the perceptions you can make, especially with regard to stress in life and how it is generally viewed in the world, you can make your life positive or negative. Impress. When you maintain a positive mentality or understanding, keep the stress response under control and work from the place where you feel happy and happy in the face of tiredness and anger. You feel in control.

Your ability to maintain a positive mentality and understanding depends on three factors:

- Your past experiences, memories, and beliefs, especially how you feel about yourself and your resources. As I briefly explained above, they affect your understanding, especially when you are in a negative mood.

- Your mood, positive or negative. I hope you have noticed the difference in your mood and emotional state as a result of your self-awareness.

- Your support infrastructure, that encourages you to have an open mind and agile body and know you've got what you need to succeed and flourish. This network encompasses how long you sleep, how well you care about yourself (e.g., fitness, diet, meditation), how good the social support group is, how often you play and joke, how well you are linked to spiritual work and values, and how you spend time in nature.

As you read on, I will provide you with tools and techniques that will help you improve your beliefs, maintain a positive spirit, and build your infrastructure. You will learn to calm your mind and calm your body to reject stress, while you learn to be sympathetic and not to judge that you feel activated. You will learn to be aware of your body's emotions, thoughts, and physiological reactions, rather than react to them, guide them, and ultimately unbind yourself. Eventually, you will learn how to access feelings of happiness, love, and compassion. To find your strength and it doesn't matter because you find your happiness.

# Part 2.	Mindfulness Meditation Exercises for Anxiety

Chapter 5.   Meditations   for   Your Body and Deep Sleep

Beginner Breathing

First, find a good sitting position that will not interfere with the process. You can use the meditation pose or sit on a chair with your hands resting on the sides and a straightened back. Do not get too comfortable though- you might 'meditate' until the next morning.

Minimize any form of distraction that can take your away attention from the meditation process. Some of these things may be a mobile phone, flashing lights, kids looking for your attention, your pet or even the weather. Find out if you should keep warm or wear loose fitted clothes before you start meditating. You may wish to close your eyes or even focus on a specific spot or object in your surroundings.

Once you are seated and comfortable with your eyes closed (or open), relax your muscles and start observing your breath. Do not try to change anything about it. The body knows the amount of air it requires. Just observe your nostrils as air flows naturally through them-in and out. The air may be cool, warm, or itchy. Every feeling is the right feeling- just observe without any judgment.

Stray thoughts may come in droves but do not hate yourself or form any resentment towards them. Just observe how your mind has the tendency of wandering and try to bring back your thoughts to breathe observation. Keep breathing and keep going deeper. Notice how the sounds around you keep drowning the deeper you take your attention into your breathing.

If stray thoughts keep recurring, notice the pattern of these thoughts. Notice what they are about, what they mostly consist of and if they are from the past or present. Bring your attention back to your breathing and continue observing your breath. At first, it may even be difficult to observe two breaths before the mind wanders. This is totally fine as it is part of the journey. Keep noticing without judgment.

Bodily distractions often come into play when meditating. Some common ones are itching, discomfort or even pain. Sometimes, different sets of emotions may arise, such as sorrow or joy, but they are impermanent-whatever they are. This should not stop you from the process. Simply observe what they are without judgment and accept whatever stories come up. Then, slowly guide yourself back to observing your breathing.

When your time runs out, bring back your attention to your body and to your surroundings. Notice how relaxed your mind is and how your breath remains the same as you open your eyes. Repeat this daily and cultivate the practice before increasing your time. You are bound to see results.

Mindful Walking Meditation

This technique comes in handy for people who are always on the move or cannot get themselves to sit and meditate. In fact, its efficiency stems from the fact that you do not need to add another routine to your daily activities to make it work. All you have to do is walk mindfully. You can always walk mindfully as you carry on with your normal routine. This practice helps to cultivate a lot of awareness as one observes within while facing the distractions of life.

It would be advisable to choose an appropriate place where you are likely to get fewer distractions as well as have good walking space. Begin with a stationary, upright position. Feel the weight of your body on your feet. You have the freedom to place your hands behind, either resting on your sides or even clasped around your chest- whatever feels comfortable. As you do this, remain relaxed and observe whatever sensations you feel objective.

Start walking using short slow steps and pay attention to the feelings that arise and pass on your feet. These feelings can vary from pain, pressure, heat or even heaviness. There is no right or wrong feeling to experience. All you have to do is observe them as they arise and pass. In this practice, the feelings one encounters as they walk are the anchor unlike in breathing meditation.

Keep walking and pay close attention to the sensations experienced on your feet as you make every step. As your foot rises and as it falls back to the ground, what do you feel? After making nonjudgmental observations, keep walking towards the chosen destination while keeping a natural and relaxed posture. When you get to the end of the walk, stand for a couple of seconds, and observe what your body feels. Before turning, center your attention back to your feet and start walking slowly again.

If the initial pace is chosen does not seem to suit the experience, feel free to switch it up a bit to the level of your comfort. You might find that walking fast works better for you! Notice how impermanent the walk is; how you keep going back and forth in the same path. You may also notice how impermanent the sensations that occur as you walk are. Just simply observe and keep practicing.

In comparison to beginner breathing, the mind is bound to wander even when doing mindful walking. This is totally fine. Noticing that your mind has wandered is half the journey. You, however, need to refocus your attention back to the next step gradually. If you notice your mind spent twenty minutes wandering, that is still fine. The fact that you noticed and refocused yourself is the most important part. Oh, and keep your eyes open!

Counting Meditation

Counting meditation is exactly as it sounds. You just need to be relaxed with your eyes closed and count up to the desired number. Ridiculous? I think not! Do you remember when we talked about the use of anchors? In this case, the numbers are your anchor. Anytime the mind decides to drift away, slowly bring back your attention to where you left off and continue counting. A practice like this can really do wonders for your attention span. Remember to observe with no judgment.

If the real intention is present when performing this practice, you will notice the intensity of the thought patterns subsides. Your thoughts will go in tandem with the counting. The more you learn to bring back your mind to focus, the more your mind detaches itself from its habitual patterns. Self-awareness develops.

These are just some of the basic meditation techniques that serve as great starters for a new meditator. If you grasp either one of these first, transitioning to the rest of the techniques taught in this book will be easy as one, two, and three.

Third Meditation

This relaxation session will help you to quickly and easily fall asleep. Relaxation is a natural sleeping technique that will allow you to gain control over some of your body's automatic responses to stressful situations.

These easy sleeping techniques can be used any time, any place, to relieve anxiety, reduce stress, fight difficult times or just to fall asleep before going to bed. I suggest you to listen to this guided meditation while lying down in your bed or in your sofa at the end of a busy day: you are going to feel refreshed and at peace once you complete the meditation.

To get the most out of this meditation session, make sure to turn off any mobile device and make yourself comfortable: it will make you relieve anxiety much faster. If, at any moment, you feel uncomfortable, feel free to change position and find a more comfortable one.

We bring attention to things as they are in the present moment, with

a receptive, open, soft attention that does not seek anything in particular, but

he receives what is there, without rejecting, without clinging ... paying attention to

what is ordinary, to this body here and now.

As if we were asking: how is the body now? ...

Breath in, feel relaxed...

breath out, feel calm...

Breath in, feel relaxed...

breath out, feel calm...

Breath in, feel relaxed...

breath out, feel calm...

Breath in, feel relaxed...

breath out, feel calm...

and rather than responding with words, letting go of thoughts, attention

connects to the body as it is. How do you feel now? The weight ... the heat ... the various

feelings of tension or relaxation ... the vibrations ...

then letting go of any comments or thoughts about the body, there is this

kind question: how is it now to be sitting here? ....

There may be stronger feelings and more nuanced sensations, parts of the body that a

I can hardly perceive, pleasant, unpleasant or neutral sensations ...

The receptive attention is ready to receive, listen, feel things as they are,

now ... (long pause)

Breath in, feel relaxed...

breath out, feel calm...

Breath in, feel relaxed...

breath out, feel calm...

Breath in, feel relaxed...

breath out, feel calm...

Breath in, feel relaxed...

breath out, feel calm...

If we distract us, if thoughts lead us into the past or the future, far from here,

when we notice this, we make a mental note: thoughts, and then

let's go back to the question, how is the body now?

Let's go back to the whole feeling of being here, now, sitting and cultivating this sense

of relaxed, open awareness, that does not look for anything, but is very awake, a lot

sensitive ..... (long break of about two minutes)

And by bringing attention to the inside of the body, we try to feel the body

from the inside: the belly ... the abdomen ... the chest area ... the throat area ... without

trying to feel anything, but be receptive to what is there. How is the body

from the inside? .... (long break)

Feeling the body from the inside, it is easy to emerge what the mood of the

moment, an emotional state, a particular mood of this moment ...

happy, sad, neutral ... tired, tense, relaxed ... we do not try to give a label,

but to experience and receive as it is the mood of this moment ...

as it manifests itself in our body ... how I feel in this

moment? ... (long pause)

We welcome what we find, be it pleasant, unpleasant or neutral ...

When thoughts, interpretations, judgments, labels arise, we do not try to

suppress them, but we do not follow them, we recognize that they are thoughts and we return to the

awareness of the body from the inside, to the observation of the mood of the

moment, trying to notice as much as possible the nuances of sensations, the quality

of what we feel now ... (long pause)

Breath in, feel relaxed...

breath out, feel calm...

Breath in, feel relaxed...

breath out, feel calm...

Breath in, feel relaxed...

breath out, feel calm...

Breath in, feel relaxed...

breath out, feel calm...

To help us maintain the stillness of the body and the stability of the mind, we can

bring attention to the lower part of the body, in the abdomen, in the thighs,

feeling precisely the contact of the body with the seat, the cushion with the earth ...

feeling the hands resting on the legs or in the womb ...

Breath in, feel relaxed...

breath out, feel calm...

Breath in, feel relaxed...

breath out, feel calm...

feeling the spine that is well erect ... and letting the attention, passing from the head, from the discursive thought, immerses itself more and more in the sensations of the body and in the state

of mind ..... (long pause)

Breath in, feel relaxed...

breath out, feel calm...

Breath in, feel relaxed...

breath out, feel calm...

Breath in, feel relaxed...

breath out, feel calm...

Breath in, feel relaxed...

breath out, feel calm...

We will notice that our perception of the body always changes, which is not possible

retaining the sensations ... we notice this fluidity this change .... nothing

it can be grasped ... the nature of the body ... and also noting the mood.

I can say restless, happy, but it's just a word.

If I try to capture the mood, what do I find?

Beyond thinking, beyond the concept ... something that escapes, that can not

to be grasped: it is a collection of sensations, perhaps memories, impressions, some

thought, emotions ... so awareness registers this elusive nature

of the state of mind .... (long break)

How do I feel now? ......

If this question is kept alive what you find changes, it is not always

equal .... (long break)

In a few moments, you will hear me count to three and you will feel blessed and awaken. 1,2,3.

Thank you.

Meditation for Becoming Tired

This meditation can be extremely helpful as you are trying to fall asleep at night. For this session, ensure that you are as comfortable as possible. You should not merely concentrate on being in a cozy sleeping position; your body should feel good as well. Allow yourself to become relaxed from your head to toes. This meditation is going to be focused on doing a body scan in order to help you feel the tension leave your body.

Make sure that you are wearing pajamas or loose clothing so that your body can fully be in a rested state. Avoid doing this in public as it might work well enough and cause you to drift off right away.

So, begin by breathing in a steady rhythm. Feel your breath come into your body through your mouth. Let it stay in your lungs for a moment before slowly releasing the air through your nose. Breathe in as I count to five, and then let it out slowly as I count from six to ten. The entire time that you are doing this, your body should be relaxed.

Breathe in for 1...2...3...4...5...6...7...8...9...10.

Then in again for one, two, three, four, five, and out for six, seven, eight, nine, ten. Now that you feel calm, it is time to start with the meditation.

We will begin with the top of your head. Allow yourself to sense the tension leave your ears. We often wear a headband of tension that radiates like a halo yet tends to squeeze our skull. Keep your forehead relaxed so that you can feel it exit your body. Try not to let your ears tense up as much as possible as well.

Next, we are going to focus more on our face. Your forehead is now relaxed, and you feel no tension in your brow. Then, bring your brows up to a high arch. The sensation may remind you of how much tension you carry in one spot of your face alone. You are starting to feel better now that your head gets into a more peaceful state.

Now is the time to stretch your jaw as wide as possible. Let it slowly come back in place, feeling all of the tension leave. It's hard to realize how tensed our jaws can be. You spend the entire day using these muscles to communicate with others. You are feeling your muscles relax now, and your face becomes completely motionless.

It is important to strengthen our facial muscles so that we can let others know how we feel without having to use any words. Nonetheless, use this time to relax. We don't have to think about that anymore. You should only focus on feeling tranquil. Your face needs to rest now.

Once your face has completely relaxed, the concentration should go down to your neck. This is another spot that holds a large amount of tension. Allow your neck to be relaxed. Place your head on soft pillows and make sure that you are not bending it too much. Your neck should be supported and not strained. It connects your head to the body, and it matters to treat it of utmost importance. Your neck gets sore when you go about your daily tasks. You may look down at your phone all day, crane your neck when reading, and stay in a slouching position, for example, and such activities can put a strain on your neck. It's important to let your neck relax as well.

Loosening up the muscles in your neck isn't as easily done as in your shoulders, though. Even if you are feeling calm, there's a good chance that you still need to loosen up your shoulders. Let them sink to the ground as if you are releasing a heavy weight from them. Keep them free from any tension the weight of the world can sometimes feel like it has been placed on our shoulders. Now, you know that you can let that go because the only thing that you need to focus on is becoming tired.

Allow your arms to relax as well. Sometimes, you won't even realize that your fists are still tightened or that your elbows are slightly bent, to the point that you are keeping your arms flexed. This can be the automatic reaction of our body when we are feeling anxious and stressed out. You need to allow these muscles to rest so that you can fully feel your arms, shoulders, and head relax, too.

We are halfway through now; that's why we are moving on to the middle of our bodies. Feel your chest calm down so that your heart can get some rest as well. Even though you can sleep, your heart will always be pumping. If you do not loosen up before bed, then your anxious heart might continue working hard all night long. Drop the tension from your chest and focus on laying flat in bed instead. Sink into the mattress and feel the soft blankets surround you.

Having a comfortable place to sleep in is when you can say that you have it all. That is the one thing that will always make us feel better no matter what the day might have held. Feel that release in your stomach now as you put attention on relaxing that part of your body. Hold your stomach in for a moment if you want as well to feel just how much tension can be in the pit of your body. Now, push your stomach out and allow it to relax along with the rest of your body.

As you are breathing in and out, fill your stomach with air. Feel how each breath makes all parts of your torso expand. Your body is powerful; you can compare it to a machine. However, even machines need to be turned off sometimes. You will never fully be off, but the muscles protecting these important organs can be relaxed so that you can get a full night of sleep.

Now, focus on letting out the tension in your back. You have already released it from your neck and shoulders, as well as your chest and stomach, but pay attention to the way that you hold your back muscles as well. There are still parts of it that need release during this body scan.

Finally, we are at the tops of our legs, thighs, and hips. Once you have stopped walking, it can feel as though that is enough to relax your body. However, the muscles on the lower half of the body can still hold tension even as you lie in bed. You might get to the point where you feel the need to shake them, move them around, and have trouble keeping them still.

Allow yourself to stay completely flat; spread your legs apart from each other and straight in front of you. When your toes are pointing up, it is harder to keep them flexed than if you are laying on your stomach with them pointed. Let the tension move out of your toes all the way from the top to the bottom.

Now, your body is completely relaxed. You are ready to fall into a deep sleep. Your mind might have been tired before starting, but you need to ensure that your body is well-rested so that you can properly fall into a deep sleep.

We are going to count to come out of this meditation. You can either go about your day more relaxed, close to nap or bedtime or fall directly into sleep. Either way, you are going to focus on keeping your body relaxed. As I count to five, breathe in through your nose, and from six to ten, out through your mouth.

One, two, three, four, five, and out, six, seven, eight, nine, ten. Count once more. 1...2...3...4...5...6...7...8...9...10.

You can use a quicker version of this body scan when you are feeling generally anxious as well. Start with the top of your head and work your way down to your toes. You will be surprised at how well it can keep you focused on relaxation and the present instead of continuing to bottle up your stress.

Guided Meditation Tips for Insomnia

Guided meditation is the form of meditation you engage in with the help of a tutor, or instructor. Ensure that you will not be disturbed during the course of this meditation.

- Lay down on your back, preferably on your bed or mat. Make sure you are comfortable on whatever you are lying on.

- Close your eyes and prepare your mind for the meditation you are about to engage in.

- Breathe in and out, ensure that your breathing out is audible such that it looks like you are breathing out heavily. Make your body feel the heaviness, after which your body will be relaxed.

- Pay more attention to your breathing, and you feel easiness. A natural breathing processes.

- At this point, you will feel your body is relaxed. Feel the way your breath travels through your lungs, and hold your breath. As this is happening, you will begin to feel relaxation in your body.

- You can begin to breathe normally right now, and as you breathe you feel your muscles, joints, and back relaxed.

- Pay more attention to your stomach area right now, where your abdominal muscles are present. Tighten the muscles in your abdomen, and hold your breath for 10 seconds and release your muscles. During this release, feel the difference between the tightness of your abdominal muscle and the relaxation of these muscles.

- Repeat the above process 5 times.

- Breathe in and out, tighten your abdomen and release it to relaxation.

Feet

- Divert your attention to your feet, and make them relaxed. The relaxation should be from your toes to your ankles. Tighten your toes and feet, and feel them become heavy and relaxed.

- Focus on your nails, feel them relaxed and let go.

- Pay attention to your thigh area, and feel them relaxed.

- Again, focus on your waist, lower and upper back, joints and feel them relaxed. You will feel the feel heavy, and very relaxed

Upper limbs

- At this point, focus your attention on your arms. Feel them heavy and relaxed.

- Get a sense of how heavy your arm is, and feel the relaxation shift to your elbow, wrist, and fingers become very relaxed.

Face, neck and facial muscles

- Shift your focus to your facial muscles, neck and face.

- Every muscle in your face, your cheeks and chin becomes relaxed, and your entire body is now relaxed.

A deeper meditation for the abdomen

- Locate your center, which is your abdominal region. Imagine there is a bowl on your abdomen. Slowly see the bowl rolling over your abdomen area, and it relaxes every muscle the bowl rolls in contact with.

- The bowl now moves slowly from your abdomen area to your right hip carefully and softly massaging the muscles of the hips it comes in contact to.

- Massaging back and forth all the muscles in your abdomen.

- The ball continues to roll over to your knee, and around your knee. You can feel the tension on your navel melting away. Roll the ball slowly to your toe, and over to your toes, from your small toes to the big toes.

Every part of your body this ball comes in contact with feel the part of your body relaxing.

- Now feel the ball begins to roll upwards away from your toes again. Massaging and reducing tension around your toes, knees, ankles and rolls over to your center, your abdominal area.

- Again, this ball rolls to your left thigh, and your knee, massaging both the back and front of your knee.

With your ball, you move this ball to wherever you choose, and how long you want it to be.

- With this ball, massage your knee, and ankle and toes. This ball touches every muscle in your toes, it gently massages them and, at this point, you feel your muscles relax.

- Feel the ball roll back up your leg, your knee and thigh muscle and arriving back at your center.

- Shift the focus of the ball to the base of your spinal cord. Allow the ball rest there for 5 seconds, and allow it move up your spine, and near your heart. At this point, you can feel the ball massaging the internal organs in your body. The ball massages the heart, and you feel relaxed.

- The ball rolls to your throat area, and the back of your neck area. You feel your neck area relaxing after the ball massages it. You feel tension reducing around your neck area.

- The ball travels down your arm, and to your wrist. The ball gently massages your wrist, and fingers.

- You feel the ball roll up your arm, to your shoulder and neck. It travels down to your elbow, forearm, and wrist and into the palm of your hands.

- Allow the ball gently massage your palm, and fingers. The ball moves up your arm, shoulder and face and as it reaches up in your face, the ball splits into a hundred tiny balls. You feel them travel around your face, to your eyes, eyebrow, cheeks, chin, teeth, tongue and teeth.

- You feel the ball massaging your face and every part of your face. At this point, you should enjoy this facial massage.

- I want you to imagine as you are lying down the ceiling of your house. Your eyes are still closed, so imagine the ceiling of your room opening itself up, and the roof also opens itself open.

- Still looking at this opening, you will see the beautiful white sky. The sky is clear, bright, and the moon is out and also full, filled with stars. This is a magical, peaceful night. You are alone, safe in the beautiful part of your house.

- Watch the twinkling and beautiful little stars, looking down on you and you are enjoying the peace of the night.

- You look again at the stars again, the little ones that are thousands of miles away are not shining so beautiful like the big star closer to you, that is looking at you directly from the sky.

- You are looking deep into galaxy, beyond time, you see a million other stars waiting for you and shining at you.

- Take a deep breath. breathe in a rich air from the infinite and beautiful galaxy filled with stars.

- Feel yourself been a part of these stars, there is no separation between you and them. Feel you are already a part of this wonderful galaxy.

- As you experience this, you become a shooting star, shining across the galaxy like others.

- Slowly you begin to fade into the sky, into the unending space and galaxy.

- You are living in the wonders of this space, where there is neither time, past or future. You feel you are the stars, the moon, and you occupy the space between the planets.

- You are floating off slowly, as you travel across this universe; you feel your body wants to drift away. You feel peace, wholeness, and love.

- When you are ready, and feel relaxed, you can let go of the galaxy. When you drift off, you will drift into a peaceful and wonderful sleep.

Guided Meditation for Insomnia in Pregnant Women

Meditation for pregnant women can seem difficult; however, the need to be relaxed is very important, to reduce tension, and frustration. Below are some tips to help you meditate as a pregnant woman.

- Pick a comfortable position, you can lie on your back, or sit upright. Ensure you feel comfortable.

- Take a deep breath, and take another deep breath for your baby.

- You are aware of your strong, beautiful and shaped body. You are aware of your baby and how beautiful the baby is.

- Ensure that you feel and observe the sensation that comes as you breathe in and out. As you are breathing in, your body is getting relaxed, and tension is reduced.

- Remember that you are pregnant and meditation can be difficult at this stage; however, take your time to be patient while meditating. Try to avoid every form of distraction around you.

- Find a quiet place to be alone for 10 – 15 minutes. Sit in an upright position, and make sure you are comfortable.

- If you are lying in bed, focus your attention on the bed, by imagining that you are sinking into the bed. And if you are sitting, create an image of your body in contact with your mattress, and also sinking into it.

- Begin to sense what it feels like to sink into your bed. Notice if you feel lighter, or heavy. Then begin awareness on your body to observe any tension and tightness around your body, from your head to toe.

- Focus your attention on any part of your body you desire, and become aware of the part of the body. Breathe in and out. Get a picture of that part, feel the tension melting away and tightness reducing.

- You can scan your body part 2times in 5 minutes. During this scan, observe and note places that are relaxed or still tight.

- Practice more breathing pattern here. Breathe in and breathe out, for the first 2 minutes, observe your breathing pattern, and focus on your breathing, without a motive to change it. You may start to notice that your breathing becomes slower on its own. You may also notice the way your body moves when you breathe. If your chest rises more than your belly does, it means your breathing is shallow.

- However, a shallow breathing is just a pattern that shows our state of relaxation. If you are relaxed, your belly will rise more than your chest.

- Place your hands on your belly, and feel your baby.

- Observe the movements in your belly with your hands,

- Think about your day, in a structured way. Look back at every activity you did during the day. Remember when your baby kicked, when you went to see the doctor, when you had a funny and interesting conversation with your friends. Be patient to watch these moments as your brain play them back for you. These flashbacks may seem long or short, it all depends on how your day went. Keep enjoying this flashback, focus your mind on it and avoid been distracted and watch as these events unfold to the present moment.

- Shift your focus back to your baby. Place your attention on your feet, toes and tell them to switch off. You can literally say the word 'switch off' out so that you feel you have told your body parts they are not needed until the next day.

- Repeat the exercise and inform your upper limbs, your arms, hands, wrist and fingers to switch off.

- Repeat your breathing exercise again.

- Place your hands on your belly, and say the following words

You are a miracle, and not a trouble.

You will allow me to have a restful night

You will be patient with me till I am awake.

You are healthy and strong."

- After saying those words, breathe in and out again for yourself and your baby.

- Imagine that your baby is falling asleep. Pay more attention on how your baby looks and the way your baby breathes.

- At this point, I believe you should be asleep. If you are not yet asleep, you can repeat the exercise and allow your mind to get relaxed.

Guided meditation for Insomnia in children

Guided meditation is a type of meditation, where there is an instructor. Little children do not have to that the knowledge to meditate on their own, so their parents can guide them into this meditation using the following.

- Welcome to your happy moment. We will start an adventure right now.

- Make sure you are lying down properly, on your bed, if you feel pain because of the way you lie down, let your parent or guardian know.

- Close your eyes properly and begin to imagine things the sun, how it is so clear and shining. Do not open your eyes.

- Start releasing your body, and everything you are thinking of. So, tighten your muscles, your arms and legs, for a few seconds.

- Let your arms get released, with your legs too. Enjoy the relaxation now, as your muscles are released

- Try the process again, tighten your arms and legs and release them later.

- Start breathing in and breathing out. Make sure you hear the sound that comes out when you breathe in and out.

- Release the air you have breathed in from your lungs, and breathe out.

- Repeat the breathing exercise, breathe in and out and relaxed.

- Now, imagine yourself in a beautiful and dark garden like the wonderland. This wonderland is dark, because it is night.

- You feel the ground is so soft that you feel like sinking into it.

- You feel a gentle and soft breeze on your face and body. The wonderland is so cool and beautiful; you don't want to leave there.

- At this point, you see your body becoming relaxed.

- You look up, and set the beautiful sunset, and the birds flying around in the wonderland.

- You continue walking; you look at the beautiful trees, with fruits on it.

- You keep walking until you see a colorful tent in front of you. The tent is the color of the rainbow. It is so beautiful; you walk into the tent.

- As you go into the tent, you see how beautiful it is. It has a beautiful sofa with the rainbow color, the wall of the tent has the pictures of all your heroes, and you like the way the tent is.

- The tents have different rooms, the living room has a Television set with your favorite cartoon, the kitchen has the pictures of your favorite food, the room has a big soft bed, you feel the softness as you touch it, and there is a big pool where you can swim before the kitchen.

- Keep walking around to see how beautiful this tent is.

- Now, you are done looking around this magical tent in your wonderland. You walk out of the tent, and you see another beautiful garden that surrounds the tent.

- This garden is so beautiful. You are walking around and you see a table with two chairs, a jug of juice, and two glass cups.

- You drink a glass of juice, and look around to see if there is anyone around you.

- You then see someone walking towards you; the person is smiling at you. The person is happy, and keeps smiling at you.

- You offer the person a glass of juice, the person receives it happily and drinks.

- You show this person around your magical tent.

- Did you have a beautiful talk with your new friend?

- You hug your visitor softly, and you watch the person go away.

- You breathe in and out and you feel happy and relaxed right now.

- At this point you are feeling sleepy, so you walk back into the tent and walk into your room to lie on your soft and rainbow color bed.

- You tuck yourself into your bed, and place your head on the soft pillow.

- You feel your body sinking into your bed. Your arms are feeling relaxed, and your hips to your toes are feeling relaxed.

- There is a window in your room, so you lie on your side to watch the beautiful dark sky and you also see the big shining star in the center of the sky.

- You smile and feel happy; you tell yourself you are a big shining star.

- You look at the other shining stars; they look beautiful just for you.

- You see them moving together fast; you wonder where they are going. They are going to the galaxy, so you decide to join them.

- You see yourself floating into the dark clouds, and far beyond the clouds, you see more stars.

- You are happy now, and very sleepy.

- You begin to drift away. You are getting sleepier, so you return to your soft bed.

- You cannot open our eyes now, because you are already deep into your sleep.

- Your mind and body are now relaxed and quiet.

- At this point, you are fast asleep.

Chapter 6.   Mindfulness Meditations

Basic Mindfulness Meditation

TIME: 15 MINUTES

Let's get right to it and give you the basics of mindfulness meditation; this exercise contains all of the fundamentals. You can come back to this exercise over and over as you continue to learn.

When learning mindfulness meditation, there are a few fundamental things you should pay particular attention to. The first is how you are sitting, which can be on the floor, on a cushion, or in a chair, and the spine should be straight but relaxed. The next thing you'll do is find your breath, wherever you are most aware of it, and simply observe it without trying to alter it. Finally, you'll move your attention to your breathing in the nose or the nostril area. Let's try it.

STEPS

1 Find a comfortable place to sit where you won't be disturbed and where you can focus on the exercise, ideally for the next 10 to 15 minutes.

2 Sit with your spine fairly straight but relaxed. You may sit with your eyes open or closed, whichever you prefer.

3 Breathe normally, noticing where you find the breath, and then bring your attention to your breath at the nostrils.

4 Be aware of your breath, and notice/follow it as you breathe in and out.

5 If or when your thoughts wander, just return your attention to your breath at the nostrils.

6 Continue to focus on your breath, perhaps sitting for 3 minutes the first time. Then, take a short break, and sit again for 5 minutes the second time. If you're feeling bold, take another very short break and then sit again for another 5 minutes.

7 Please congratulate yourself and go about your day. You may find it useful to keep notes as to when you meditated, for how long, and how it went.

Mindfulness Exercise 1

In this exercise, you take the same stance of lying down in a darkened room or at least one with subdued light. Make sure that there is nothing that will interrupt your chain of thought. That means turning off the TV and it also means closing the window, if there is outside noise. Make sure that your clothing is completely comfortable because this time, instead of thinking of nothing, you are going to be concentrating on something in particular and the last thing that you need is clothing that hurts you or that is constrictive.

Close your eyes and relax. Count to ten thinking of nothing at all. Then, start to breathe in through your nose deeply and hold the breath for a couple of moments, breathe out through the mouth. The idea of this exercise is that you concentrate your mind totally on your breathing. Feel the air rushing in through your nose, going down into your chest, and feel the stillness when you hold your breath. Then, breathe out through the mouth and feel the air expelling itself from your body right down from the abdomen up to the chest and then out through your mouth. Concentrate totally on your breathing. Repeat the exercise ten times if you have the time to do this.

What you are doing is becoming aware of your breathing. Instead of filling your mind with whatever the troubles of the day are, you are mentally stepping away from outside influence and enjoying the moment with breathing and simply concentrating on what you are actually doing, rather than having your mind diverted by thoughts.

Mindfulness Exercise 2

While in a relaxed state of mind, lying in the same position on your back, close your eyes and feel your feet. Tense them so that your thought is directed toward your feet. Then feel them become heavy and relax. Work through all of the different parts of the body, tensing the part of the body before relaxing and letting it feel heavy.

The parts of the body that are relevant to this exercise are:

➢   Toes, calf, knee, thigh

➢   Waist, hips and abdomen

➢   Chest, neck and head

When you have covered the whole body in your meditative thinking, relax for a moment and breathe deeply, in through the nose and out through the mouth. Finishing off your exercise, get up very slowly. Never jump back into life straight away, but let your body go at its own speed.

Mindfulness Exercise 3

Make full use of all your sensory perceptions. Don't take into account only what you can see or hear; feel it, taste it, breathe it in. Observe your surroundings without judging them – just take them in as they are. Let your mind go blank. Now close your eyes and then pick out a single sense – start with your nose. Take in all the smells around you. Mentally list them out, from the wet grass to the stinky hosepipe, leave out nothing. Now slowly move from your sense of smell to what you can hear – list that out one by one. From the sound of the cars splashing the puddles to the crickets chirping, don't leave out anything. When you list the smells and the sounds, keep your eyes closed.

Now open them, and take in what you see. List it out, from the beam of sunlight shining bright through the trees to the glare of the car's windscreen. Now move from your sight to your touch – list out what you can feel. From the blade of grass crunched beneath your feet to the way, the sunglasses feel perched on your nose, leave nothing out.

Once you've listed out all the different things your five senses perceive, pick out those things – only those things – that you appreciate. Ignore that which irritates you and think only of what makes you happy. Remember, you aren't actively looking for something to appreciate. You are picking what you like from what you already have felt. There is an active difference between the two.

This is a stress-reducing exercise that helps you remain rooted in the singular moment you are experiencing.

Mindfulness Exercise 4

Draw your attention to the soles of your feet. If you are feeling distracted or irritated and anxious, this is a good exercise to calm down and bring your attention back to a single strain of thought. Gather all your attention and direct it towards the soles of your feet.

Now slowly move your toes one by one – take time to do it and feel each and every movement. Move your attention from one toe to the other and give each finger the full focus it deserved. Then from the toes, drag your focus to the other sensory perceptions in the area – feel the cotton of your socks resting

against your skin and the cut of the shoes/sandals you are
wearing. Feel the earth beneath you or the sand beneath your
toes – pay attention to every pebble or grain of sand that
grates against your skin.

As you are giving attention to all these things, breathe in and
out deeply. Keep your attention focused on your feet, but draw
in a breath deeply and let it out slowly. Do this continuously
for a few minutes until you find yourself calming down or your
mind blanking anything but your feet.

Mindfulness Exercise 5

When you are waiting – in line, for a friend to show up, for a
movie to start – don't get irritated. Instead of being annoyed
that the instance you are waiting for is going to take time to
begin, take the moment you do have it hand and use it. In the
fast, rushed lifestyle you lead, these few minutes are actually a
calm respite for you – treat it as such. You don't have to cater
to someone, you don't have worry about fulfilling a
responsibility and you have – literally – nothing to do except
wait. There is absolutely no obligation in those two minutes;
take them to focus on your breathing. Mindfully inhale and
then exhale; do some people watching or focus on what your
different senses are telling you – how the wind is cold, how the
bag feels warm against your side and how the birds are
chirping, and the smell of coffee is overpowering. Take the

time to savor the moment and calm your stress over waiting down.

Just Breathe

Time 5 Minutes

Best for Preventing chronic stress

One of the major tools available to you for a mindful state is your breath. Remember that the objective of a mindfulness practice is to turn off your mind and allow yourself to be still. Focusing only on your breath allows that to happen. When you focus on your physical act of breathing, it is more difficult to go into your thoughts. There are several different ways to explore your breath as a pathway to being in the present moment.

1. Find a quiet place where you can comfortably sit or lie down.

2. Start by breathing normally. Notice how it feels. Feel the warmth as air enters your nostrils and throat. Notice where you feel your breath in your body—your chest or your abdomen.

3. Follow the breath as it enters your lungs and then feel the sensations as you follow it from your lungs out through your nose or mouth. Let all your attention focus on the breath. Notice as one breath ends and the next begins.

4. Sense the breath as a quality of motion. Notice how it moves in the different parts of your body as you breathe in a steady rhythm.

5. Now inhale through your mouth while counting to 4: 1, 2, 3, 4. Then count backward on the exhale: 4, 3, 2, 1. Try to breathe very slowly. The goal is to focus on the sensations that you feel at each point. Do this for 5 minutes.

6. After several days, increase the length of time you inhale, exhale, and hold the breath. Start by holding the breath as you count to 5. Slowly exhale as you count to 5. Do this for 5 minutes. After several days, increase gradually to a total of 10 minutes. Practice this exercise twice each day.

Harnessing Your Breath

If you breathe more deeply and let the area around your stomach expand, you are pulling the air in and pushing it out with your diaphragm. When you catch your mind wandering, gently bring your focus back to your breath. Breathe in through your nose slowly and feel the sensation of the air as it travels to your lungs. To bring in as much oxygen as possible, be aware of the point where you need to breathe more deeply. Place one hand on your stomach and the other on your chest. As you take a breath in, you should feel the hand on your stomach rise beyond the other one, and when you breathe out, it should be lower. Doing this guarantees that you are getting the full benefit of the breath.

Calm Eating

Time 10 Minutes

Best for Conscious consumption

You may find that you don't eat in a mindful way, hurrying through meals without savoring the flavors and textures of the food. In this exercise, you will use all your senses to experience food.

1. Get an orange or another juicy fruit that you like.

2. Pick up the orange. Look at it. Look at its roundness. See the texture and all the tiny creases in the skin. Notice the variations in color, as if you were going to paint it from memory.

3. Feel the texture of the skin. What does it feel like to run your fingers over it? Concentrate on the sensations on your fingertips. Staying focused, tear a piece of the skin from the top of the orange. Feel the tension on your fingernails and the change in pressure as the skin gives way. Experience the difference between the toughness of the skin and the softness of the flesh under it.

4. Bring the orange to your nose. Can you smell anything? Tear a larger strip of skin. Now smell the open orange. Let the layers of fragrance linger in your nose. Note the variations in fragrance as minutes go by.

5. Let all thoughts drift away. If you find yourself thinking of something, redirect your focus to the orange. Now taste the juice. What sensations take the stage? Let the layers of flavor wander over your tongue. Is it sweet? Is it bitter? Now take a small bite of the orange. Chew it until there is no pulp left.

6. Squeeze the orange, allowing the juice to fall into a glass. Feel the pressure on the palm of your hand. Watch the juice and its motion. Listen to the sounds. Watch the flow of the juice. Now drink the juice. Again, pay attention with all five senses, one at a time. When you follow these steps, you are eating in the moment.

Come to Your Senses

Time 5 Minutes

Best for Staying present

With this exercise, you will learn how to use all your senses to still your mind. Paying attention to all your senses allows you to be present in the moment. This exercise will enable you to lower your stress by getting out of your head and just being with yourself and your experience. You can practice every day for about five minutes. Because it will relax you, you may take more time, and that is fine.

1. Pick the day and time when you will do this sensory experiment and choose where you want to do it. It can be

where you live or in another location, perhaps in a city or in the country or at a beach.

2. Find a comfortable place to sit. Close your eyes and open yourself up to any sensation through any one of your senses. Listen to any sounds. Are they high sounds, scratchy sounds, chirpy sounds? Let your mind just focus on listening. Listen to the sounds change as one comes into focus and as another takes over. Pay attention to any sounds in the background. Is there a plane flying overhead, or are there horns honking? Is it quiet?

3. Move your awareness to any scents. What do you smell? Try to notice each scent as though you have never smelled it before. If you are in the city, do you smell car exhaust? If you are in the country, do you smell trees or grass? You may have to make a conscious effort because you may not usually pay attention to smell unless it is overpowering and bad.

4. Open your eyes. Look around with intention. Notice the shapes, the colors. Take in the sight of something as though it is the first time you have ever seen it.

5. Now touch an object or surface. Notice the texture. Is it smooth? Bumpy?

6. As you move through this exercise, notice any thoughts that float in. As with the other exercises, observe your thoughts and let them go. Come back to your senses.

A Walk in the Park

Time 5 Minutes

Best for Mindfulness while walking

The art of reducing stress is to stay as mindful as you can throughout the day. Doing this when you walk is a wonderful way to continue to stay relaxed and to reduce stress. Normally, when you are walking, you are just thinking of getting to where you are going, and your mind is filled with thoughts of the past or future. The goal of this exercise is to keep you in the present and allow your mind to be open to the sensory experiences of walking. There are a lot of moving parts when you walk. You probably never focus on the feeling of your feet touching the ground or the brush of your pants or skirt on your legs. Try this exercise with different types of walking, such as rushing to be somewhere, or when you are angry, or when you are filled with joy. This exercise helps you clear your mind, and you can practice it several times a day or whenever you go for a walk.

1. Start by just standing still. Notice the weight on your feet. Notice your balance. Do you make slight adjustments to stay balanced? Feel the weight of your body on your legs, knees, and ankles.

2. Start walking slowly. Feel the weight on your foot. Notice how your foot touches the ground and stays in contact until you lift it up. Can you notice any other sensations; like the way

your feet feel in your shoes? Are they very comfortable, or do they pinch your toes?

3. Notice what your ankle feels like when the ball of your foot touches the ground. How do your thighs or calves feel as you lift your feet and put them down?

4. Pay attention to your knees. What do you feel? Do they ache or feel strong? Do you feel how they help propel your legs?

5. Explore any other physical sensations from your hips and the rest of your body. Notice any thoughts or emotions that arise.

A Touching Moment

Time 5 Minutes

Best for Building sensory awareness through touch

As you continue to explore your senses in the present moment, this exercise will focus on touch. Tactile sensations are the most primitive of all senses. It is the first sense an infant experiences when held by his mother. The sense of touch often dominates over all other senses. This exercise will help you achieve mindfulness through touch. Throughout the exercise, when you find your mind wandering or thinking, note it and let it go.

1. Choose a place to do these explorations. Outdoors might provide more variety, but you can also do them indoors. Stay as focused as you can on the journey you are taking now.

2. Start by standing. Feel your feet connecting you with the ground. Feel the pressure on your toes, on the balls of your feet, on your heels. Concentrate on the sensation. Feel the weight of your clothes, your chest pressing against your shirt as you breathe in. Now, feel the weight of your shoulders as you stand straight. Feel the air entering your lungs, then leaving. Feel any sensation on your face.

3. Begin to walk, and as you walk, touch your legs with your hands. What is the texture of your clothing? Rough? Smooth? Rippled?

4. Find a place to sit. Feel the weight of your body settling onto that place. As you sit, do you feel something hard? Soft? If you are on a chair, what does your back feel as it leans against the chair? If you are sitting on a bed, how does it feel as you sink into the mattress surface?

5. Wrap your arms around yourself. What do your hands feel? Are you wearing a shirt? Is it soft or is it starchier? How do your hands feel as they clasp your arms? What do your arms feel as they are gripped by your hands? Do they feel warm? Are they comforting?

6. Now touch your face. Note the texture. Is it soft? Stubbly?

7. If you are inside, go to the refrigerator. Take out anything cold and hold it. Feel the cold on your hands. Take a towel. Feel the texture. Soak the towel with warm water. Feel the warmth of the water and the softer texture of the towel.

Body Scan

Time 5 to 7 Minutes

Best for Calming your body

One of the key mechanisms for clearing your mind of stress is to focus on your body, because when you are focusing on your body, it is very difficult to focus on your thoughts. This exercise targets the tension you hold in your muscles and allows you to release it.

1. Start by lying or sitting in a comfortable position.

2. Take a slow, deep breath in through your nose. Feel your breath go deeper and let your stomach expand as you breathe in. Slowly let your breath out through your mouth. Do this three times.

3. Notice any physical sensations such as warmth, tingling, or chills. Pay attention to each sensation separately as you notice it. If you feel tension, send it a message to let go. Focus on your hands. Feel the sensations in your fingertips, then your fingers, then your knuckles.

4. Take a deep breath. Feel your stomach expand as you breathe. Let your breath out slowly. Focus your attention on your wrists. Release any tension you feel. Now concentrate on your forearms. Let the tension go.

5. Pay attention to your elbows, the back of your upper arms, and the front of your upper arms. Concentrate now on your biceps and then your shoulders. Continue to take slow, deep breaths.

6. Center your attention on your neck. What sensations do you experience: warmth, tension, tingling? Move up your neck to the base of your skull. Concentrate now on your scalp. Come back down your neck to your shoulders. Slowly move to your upper back, then your lower back.

7. Take a moment. If there is stress there, let it go.

8. Now go to your chest. Take a breath and let the tension go. Now, slowly, focus on your abdomen and your core. Bring attention to your hips. Release any tension. Then concentrate on your upper thighs and now your knees and then slowly move to your calves. See if there is tension in your shins or your ankles. Focus on the soles of your feet, the top of your feet, and your toes. Let all your tension drift away.

Love Begins with Yourself

Time 10 Minutes

Best for Building a strong relationship with yourself

Loving-kindness meditation is the concept of maintaining a mental state of unselfish and unconditional kindness to all beings. To start with loving-kindness, you must begin with yourself. At first, you may feel as though you are going through the motions of feeling self-love. After a short while, though, you will find that the loving thoughts you have been giving yourself start becoming part of your unconscious mind, and then they become part of you.

1. Start by sitting comfortably in a quiet place. Take slow, deep breaths, feeling your stomach expand as you breathe

2. Picture an image of yourself at any time you felt your own self-worth. If you can't remember, think of a time when you were loved by another. Try to be open to it and let the warmth of that feeling spread through your body.

3. Now picture someone who loves or has loved you very much standing on your left side. It could be a relative, a partner, or a child. Picture another person who loves you on your right side.

4. Imagine yourself surrounded by all the people who care about you. Feel their love and say:

- May I be safe and healthy
- May I be happy

5. Now picture the people around you. Send love out to them. Say:

- May you accept yourself just as you are
- May you be safe and healthy
- May you be happy

6. Picture a person you do not have a connection to, perhaps a stranger. Repeat the words. Now picture someone you do not like. Repeat the words. If this is difficult, come back to the image of yourself and repeat the words.

Tense and Release

Time 5 to 7 Minutes

Best for Total relaxation

This exercise is a wonderful way to create a relaxation response to counter the stress response. It takes time to retrain your body's response to tension and stress. When you practice every day, your body develops a memory of being relaxed that will become automatic.

1. Find a quiet place. You can do this exercise either lying down or sitting in a chair.

2. Take a deep breath in through the nose, letting your stomach expand to let your lungs expand fully. Exhale slowly through the mouth. Start with your hands. Make tight fists. Squeeze them for a count of 10, or until it burns a little bit, and release them.

3. Flex your forearms by extending your arms with your hands tilted back toward your head. Hold until you feel a slight burning sensation. Now relax your arms.

4. Flex your biceps. Hold them as if you are a bodybuilder. Hold them for a count of 10. And then release. Lift your shoulders up toward your ears. Hold for a count of 10. Now release.

5. Now, tense the muscles in your face. Make the funniest face that you can and hold it until it burns. Relax your face. Feel the difference between when you are tensed and when you are relaxed.

6. Take another deep breath. Flex your core. Press your arms against your sides and push in while you do a partial sit-up. Feel the muscles tighten in your abdomen. Hold it until it burns slightly. Now release.

7. Take another breath. Flex your buttocks, hold, then release. Extending one leg at a time, flex your thigh, your quadriceps muscle. Hold until you feel tension, then release. Be careful not to get a cramp. Repeat with the other leg. Take another deep breath.

8. Now flex your calf muscles. Point your toes back toward your head. You can do both at the same time. Hold and then release. Finally, flex your toes. Hold for a count of 10, then

release. Take another breath. Again, note the difference between when you are tensed and when you are relaxed.

Mindful Indulgences

Time 15 Minutes

Best for Relaxing activities

This exercise guides you to stay in the present moment with your body during a relaxing, indulgent activity—in this case, taking a warm bath. Make a list of things you find completely pleasurable. If a relaxing bath is not on your list, use this exercise to guide your own pleasurable activities. Be sure to pay attention to your body and all your senses during the activity. Be completely self-indulgent.

1. Choose a time when you can disconnect from all other distractions. To do this exercise properly, you must be totally self-indulgent. You can't hold back.

2. Start running a bath by choosing the perfect temperature for the water.

3. Turn the lights down. If you have some candles, bring them in and light them.

4. As the water fills the tub, let it flow over your hand. Focus on the sensation of the warmth and notice the water pressure. Is it strong? What does it sound like?

5. Your thoughts of the day may be racing around your head with the plans you need to make for tomorrow. When you catch yourself thinking or planning, just notice it and direct your attention back to the sensations.

6. Would you care for a cool drink in your bath or a warm cup of tea? If you choose tea, pay attention to the steps involved in preparing it. Notice the sound of the teakettle as you open it. Hear the sound of the water coming from the faucet to fill it. Notice the weight of the kettle and how it feels when you place it on the stove or connect it to the wall socket. Smell the tea before you brew it. Stay with the sense of it.

7. If you prefer a cold drink, feel the temperature of the glass on your hand. Listen as you pour the liquid into the glass.

8. When you take a sip, feel the sensation on your lips and in your throat.

9. For any other treat you may like, go through the same process. See, listen, smell, feel, and then taste. At each moment, stay focused on the sensory input. By staying present in the moment, you will find yourself enjoying your favorite activities even more.

This Will Put You to Sleep

Time 5 to 10 Minutes

Best for Getting to sleep

Do you ever have trouble falling asleep? If not, you are lucky. A National Sleep Foundation poll found that 63 percent of women and 54 percent of men experienced insomnia at least a few nights per week. If insomnia is ever a problem, this brief body scan can really help. The steps in this exercise will enhance your mindfulness practice, and it can also help send you to sleep.

1. As you lie in bed, close your eyes. Inhale, using slow, deep breaths. Let your stomach expand as you breathe in. Exhale slowly. Do this five times, very slowly. Your mind will probably wander as you do this. If so, note it and bring your focus back to your breathing. You may need to do this several times. Just breathe.

2. Focus on your body, starting with your toes. If you feel any tension, let it go. Move your focus slowly to your ankles and feet. Same there; if you feel any tension, give it a signal to let it go. Make sure you don't rush through this, as it is important to take time.

3. As you move up your body to your calves, knees, and thighs, note any tension and let it go.

4. Move up to your hips and slowly to your lower back. Slowly move your focus to your upper back and shoulders. Visualize any tension drifting away and being replaced with calm. Move to your chest and your shoulders. Be aware of how they feel as you tense and release your muscles.

5. Focus on your neck and head. Release any tension from each part of your face and your scalp. Move to your upper arms, your triceps, then your biceps, your forearms, your hands, and your fingers. Take slow, deep breaths.

6. After you've scanned your entire body, focus your awareness completely on your breath. Breathe in, slowly and deeply. Then breathe out fully. During each breath start counting very slowly backward from five. 5 . . . 4 . . . 3 . . . Between each number give yourself a sleepy suggestion, such as, I will be asleep soon. My eyes are getting heavy. I feel my muscles getting heavy. My body is relaxed.

7. When you catch yourself thinking about something instead of focusing on your breath, notice that it is happening, and start counting down again from 5. If you make it down to 1 a couple of times, you will soon be asleep. Good night.

Mindfulness on the Go

Mindfulness can help you stay calm, perform better in all aspects of your life, and reduce stress. One benefit of this process is that you can take it with you wherever you go and in whatever you do.

Mindfulness Morning

Time 5 minutes each morning

Best for Starting your day

Starting your morning the right way can set the tone for the rest of the day. Mindfulness is a great tool for stabilizing your moods and your responses to the stress of life. During an average day, you will be bombarded by many stimuli. You will face stresses and struggles. It takes a conscious effort to balance yourself in the face of all of them. You may find yourself reacting without thinking, acting on autopilot, and ending up feeling drained.

Studies have shown that the way you center yourself in the morning can build a buffer for you that makes it all easier. This exercise will show you how to get your day off to a positive start.

1. Instead of jumping out of bed immediately, give yourself a few minutes to transition from sleep to wakefulness.

2. Attend to your needs, then perform a mental check of things you must do in the morning, such as pack lunches for the kids. You should plan this exercise around those duties.

3. Find a quiet place and take slow, deep breaths. Concentrate on the present moment and let go of all the thoughts about the coming day. Do this for 5 minutes.

4. Think of one thing you are grateful for. Bask in the glow of that thought. Focus on your gratitude as you breathe.

5. As you move forward with the rest of your day, incorporate your awareness into each activity. If you shower or take a bath,

do it consciously, feeling the sensations and listening to the sounds.

6. If you are making breakfast, pay attention to the sounds, smells, and textures of each task. If you are cracking an egg, listen to the shell breaking. Feel the pressure on your fingers when it cracks. Hear the sizzle when it hits the frying pan.

7. Mindfully go through the rest of the breakfast, being aware of taste and texture.

8. After the meal, hear the sound and splash of the water as you wash your plate. The goal is to stay aware and focused to clear your mind of clutter. When you accomplish this, your mind will be more effective throughout the day.

9. Getting your children ready for school can make it difficult to maintain your focused state. Before reacting to a demand or to resistance to one of your demands, identify your emotions. If you become frustrated or angry, recognize the emotion and its effect on your body. Neutralize it by taking three deep breaths. Think of what you need to make happen, and do not react.

Using Social Media

Time 5 Minutes

Best for Preventing jealousy and envy

Social media has revolutionized the world. The different platforms—Facebook, Snapchat, Instagram, Twitter—have also created a number of problems. One problem is that they can make you feel bad. People usually only post pictures of times when they are happy. If you happen to be feeling bad, you may start comparing your life to your perception of theirs, and you may feel bad unnecessarily. Mindfulness is a wonderful antidote to the toxic effects of social media.

Beating the Commuter Blues

Time The length of your commute

Best for Traveling to and from work

Fifty-four percent of Americans commute to work. Studies have shown that getting to the train on time, dealing with crowded cars, and putting up with other passengers who may be unpleasant all create stress. If you drive to work, traffic jams and rude drivers also put you under stress. There is not much you can do about changing the stressful conditions of a daily commute, but you do have control over your response to them. Mindfulness is a very effective way to balance your mood during what may be one of the most stressful activities of the day.

Working It Out

Time 30 to 60 Minutes

Best for Exercising

The gym is an important place for many people. Some people use it because it feels good. Others exercise because it keeps them healthy. Still others use the gym to release stress. How do you use your gym time? Do you rush through your workout to finish it as soon as you can, or do you savor it? Adding mindfulness can add depth to the experience, which allows you to enjoy it in a different way.

Peaceful Shopping

Time 5 to 60 Minutes

Best for Shopping at stores

I am guessing you spent more time visiting stores 10 years ago than you do now. With everything from clothing to groceries available online, there are fewer and fewer reasons to go to a store. Too often shopping is a race against time: You need to get home to make dinner or you have to get back to your office. It is rare to savor the moments. Other times it can be annoying to not find the item you are looking for, or every size but yours is available. If you are in a department store, you may not even know which department to go to. If you do still shop the old-fashioned way, or you would like a less stressful experience, perform this mindfulness exercise.

Ho, Ho, Holidays

Time 5 Minutes

Best for Holiday events

The holidays are a complex time with much to do. Preparations, buying presents, and attending parties take time and can put pressure on you. Families come together during the holidays, and family interactions are rarely simple; there is closeness and sometimes there is tension. Alternatively, one may not have a family, and the holidays are hard because of that. All of this is under the guise of a holiday that should be joyous. Mindfulness is a wonderful tool to keep you in a positive frame of mind.

Everyday People

Time 5 Minutes

Best for Calming down during difficult interactions

Some people interact with others as though they have a chip on their shoulder. They might be aggressive, unreasonable, insensitive, or provocative. Being in their presence creates stress. They are difficult to deal with. If someone acts in a difficult manner around you, you might feel angry or hurt or upset. Those emotions make you react. Being mindful allows you to avoid reacting by detaching from those emotions. Once your emotions do not control your behavior, you will have more options for handling difficult people.

Getting the Job Done

Time 5 Minutes

Best for Household chores

How do you feel about doing chores? If something has to get done, do you get it done? The word chore implies that the task is mandated rather than chosen. The purpose of this exercise is, in part, to help you get chores done more easily. The other is to help you do them mindfully. Mindfulness connects you fully to the activity in which you are engaged. You become part of it.

Give Yourself a Break

Time 5 Minutes

Best for Enjoying time off

Downtime is defined as leisure time, such as having time off between periods of work. Our lives are very busy. You may not even experience much downtime in your life. Yet it is critically important for your body and for your brain to take a break. Stress is caused by having more to do than time in which to do it. It is also caused by the thoughts that constantly bombard you about everything you have to do. Mindfulness allows you to experience life more fully without judgments or distracting thoughts. Applying this exercise to your downtime has great rewards, such as increasing the enjoyment you feel.

Mindful Slumber

Time 5 Minutes

Best for Preparing for sleep

You spend over one-third of your life in your bed. It is a place of dreams and rejuvenation. You most likely see it as just your bed. You stay up until you go to bed, and you get up and do everything you do in the day, and then you go to bed. One of the beautiful attributes of mindfulness is that it allows you to savor life. So often we rush and rush and never stop to feel what we are experiencing. This segment is to help you use mindfulness to appreciate this nightly companion.

Discover the Thinker

TIME: 15 MINUTES

In this exercise, we're going to focus on meeting your mind.

I remember distinctly when I was first training in mindfulness meditation, there was an inner shift in which I became aware of my thinking and my mind. It was not like I hadn't had thoughts or been aware of them before, but in that moment, I became very aware of my mind and the thoughts running through it. I could begin to observe them and work with them. It was a bit startling initially, but very useful. That's what I mean by "discovering the thinker."

STEPS

1 Find a comfortable place to sit where you can focus undisturbed.

2 Sit with your spine fairly straight and your eyes open or closed, whichever is easiest.

3 Breathe normally, noticing where you find the breath, and then bring your attention to your breath at the nostrils.

4 Be aware of your breath and follow it as you breathe in and out.

5 Begin to be aware of and pay attention to your thinking. Notice the thoughts that you're having and the range of topics in their discursive, or meandering, nature.

6 Try to become aware of the thoughts and where they are coming from. If you can do this, then you will discover your mind. It may take several tries. Stay with this step, as you hopefully find your thoughts and your mind. If not, you can come back to it again later.

7 Sit for a while more and let everything go. Simply be aware of the breath at the nostrils, sit for a while more, and then take a few moments to slowly transition out of meditation.

Observe Non-judgmentally

TIME: 20 TO 30 MINUTES

We are learning important basics, like how to sit, keep our back straight but relaxed, be aware of our breath and focus it at the nose or nostrils, and begin to locate our mind and be aware of our thoughts. This next step follows logically from what we have just done in becoming aware of our mind and our thinking. We are used to being carried along by random, discursive, and incessant thoughts—now we will take a step back and examine how our thoughts are often very critical and judgmental in nature.

STEPS

1 Find a comfortable place to sit, where you can focus undisturbed.

2 Sit with your spine straight, but relaxed, eyes open or closed.

3 Breathe normally, and then bring your attention to your breath at the nostrils.

4 Be aware of your breath and notice it as you breathe in and out.

5 Now, pay attention to your thinking. Notice your thoughts, the range of topics, and your thoughts' discursive nature.

6 Become aware of your thoughts and the judgments that are involved. Are the judgments about yourself, others, or both? What are the critical thoughts that you are having, and how do they make you feel?

7 Can you merely have your observations and thoughts without the judgments? Can you observe your thoughts and notice if they are critical, and if they are, pause and stop the criticism? Can you give yourself a bit of space, or step back (figuratively speaking), and merely observe things without judging? This is the goal. Try this several times, with short breaks in between. If

you catch yourself judging, just note and drop it, and return to the meditation.

8 Sit for a while more while letting everything go. Simply be aware of the breath at the nostrils. Sit for a while more, and then slowly come out of meditation.

9 You may wish to make some ongoing notes, such as where and when the meditation occurred, how long it took, what breaks you took, and what you noticed as you did it.

Meditation for Happiness & Peace Within

This practice is designed to restore happiness and peace from within. The easiest way to practice it is to adopt an easy pose while keeping your spine straight. Ensure that the chin is in and the chest out.

-To warm up, start chanting a mantra such as 'Aum' for about 10 seconds. You should chat through the couch, as you keep your mouth slightly open. You should allow the breath to come out only out of the nostrils.

-Chant this mantra for about 5 times and then accelerate your chant faster, in a bid to recite a chant after every 3-5 seconds. The duration for this meditation can range from 1-2 minutes until you experience your required state for happiness.

However, if you start to cough when in meditation practice, just allow the coughing to end naturally since your thyroid is trying to adjust to the pressure. Chanting a positive affirmation or mantra in the correct way should give you happiness and peace within your troubled mind.

Loving Kindness Meditation

This technique forms one of the popular practices and focuses on loving energy towards your mind or towards other people. This practice is important in making you experience the warm feelings of loving kindness, on top of regular benefits of meditation. You can follow this simple technique for happiness.

-Locate a silent or relaxing place and sit in your most comfortable posture. Keep your eyes closed, muscles relaxed and then take slow and deep breaths.

-Imagine that you are witnessing a perfect emotional or physical wellness or inner peace. Also imagine that you are experiencing complete love and that you are thankful to yourself for everything you are. Acknowledge that you are right, in whatever state that you are.

-Make 3-4 repetitions of positive, reassuring phrases to yourself, any mantra that you find relaxing. You can adopt some affirmations such as "May I be happy", "May I be safe", "May I be peaceful, healthy, and strong." Or "May I give and receive acceptance today".

-Bask in this experience for some time, redirecting your feelings back to your mantra in case your mind seems to wander. Try to receive as many benefits from these feelings of loving kindness.

-Based on your preference, you may choose to stay in this kind of meditation, or alternatively, shift your focus to those people that you treasure. Begin with a close friend or a relative, and try to feel your love or gratitude for them. You may decide to repeat your phrase that contributes to feelings of loving kindness within you.

-After holding these positive feelings towards a person, now extend the loving kindnesses to other important people from your life into your consciousness.

-Examine these people one by one, and then envision them with the same perfect wellness and inner peace.

-From here, you can further extend to another group of people such as neighbors, acquaintances or other people you share similar ideas. These may include people you are often in a conflict, so that you can find ways of greater peace or forgiveness.

-After you are done with meditation, open your eyes and then acknowledge the possibility of revisiting that wonderful feeling in your entire day. You can memorize the feelings of loving kindness, and then revisit the feeling through deep breaths and focus shift in a certain entire day.

The best way to start this meditation practice is from you as the subject before extending to other people. Although directing the meditation to troublesome people may allow room for forgiveness, it takes a lot of patience to achieve this. To help control the time you spend during meditation, you may set a timer to about 4-5 minutes sessions.

Second Meditation

This relaxation session will help you to quickly and easily heal yourself. Relaxation is a natural self-healing technique that will allow you to gain control over some of your body's automatic responses to stressful situations.

These easy self-healing techniques can be used any time, any place, to relieve anxiety, reduce stress, fight difficult times or just to fall asleep. I suggest you to listen to this guided meditation while lying down in your bed or in your sofa at the end of a busy day: you are going to feel refreshed and at peace once you complete the meditation.

To get the most out of this meditation session, make sure to turn off any mobile device and make yourself comfortable: it will make you relieve anxiety much faster. If, at any moment, you feel uncomfortable, feel free to change position and find a more comfortable one.

I breathe in, and I am aware of the air that enters, and I am aware of my breath coming out.

Inhaling, I rejoice in the inspiration. Exhaling, I rejoice in exhaling.

Inhaling, I feel so full of life. Breathing out, I smile to life in and around me myself.

Inhaling, I am aware of my whole body. Breathing out, I smile at all of my body.

Breathing in, I am aware of my whole body. Exhaling, I let all go tensions from my body.

Breath in, feel relaxed...

breath out, feel calm...

Breath in, feel relaxed...

breath out, feel calm...

Breath in, feel relaxed...

breath out, feel calm...

Breathing in, I know spring has come. Exhaling, I see flowers bloom.

Inhaling, I see my heart like a flower. Exhaling, I let my heart go open like a flower.

Inhaling, I see my father in every cell of my body. Exhaling, I smile at my own father in every cell of my body.

Inhaling, I invite my father to rejoice with me of the breath that comes in. Exhaling, invite

my father to rejoice with me of the breath that comes out.

Inhaling, I feel so light. Do you feel the same thing, dad? Exhale, me I feel so free. Dad, do you feel free like me?

Inhaling, I notice the presence of my mother in every cell of my body Exhaling, I smile to my mother in me.

Inhaling, I invite my mother who is in me to rejoice with me of the breath that enters, Exhaling I invite my mother who is in me to rejoice with me of the breath that goes out.

Breath in, feel relaxed...

breath out, feel calm...

Breath in, feel relaxed...

breath out, feel calm...

Breath in, feel relaxed...

breath out, feel calm...

Inhaling, I feel so light, Mom, you feel light as you are myself? Breathing in, I feel so free, Mother, do you feel free as I am?

My mother and I rejoice together to breathe together. My mother and I enjoy the exhalation together.

My father and I rejoice in the inspiration of my father, and I enjoy the exhalation together.

Breathing in, I see my heart like a flower.

Exhaling, I let my heart go open like a flower.

Breath in, feel relaxed...

breath out, feel calm...

Breath in, feel relaxed...

breath out, feel calm...

I breathe in, and I am aware of the air that enters, and I am aware of my breath coming out.

Inhaling, I rejoice in the inspiration. Exhaling, I rejoice in exhaling.

Inhaling, I feel so full of life. Breathing out, I smile to life in and around me myself.

Inhaling, I am aware of my whole body. Breathing out, I smile at all of my body.

Breathing in, I am aware of my whole body Exhaling, I let all go tensions from my body.

Breathing in, I know spring has come. Exhaling, I see flowers bloom.

Inhaling, I see my heart like a flower. Exhaling, I let my heart go open like a flower.

Breath in, feel relaxed...

breath out, feel calm...

Breath in, feel relaxed...

breath out, feel calm...

Breath in, feel relaxed...

breath out, feel calm...

Inhaling, I see my father in every cell of my body. Exhaling, I smile at my own father in every cell of my body.

Inhaling, I invite my father to rejoice with me of the breath that comes in. Exhaling, invite

my father to rejoice with me of the breath that comes out.

Inhaling, I feel so light. Do you feel the same thing, dad? Exhale, me I feel so free. Dad, do you feel free like me?

Inhaling, I notice the presence of my mother in every cell of my body Exhaling,

I smile to my mother in me.

Inhaling, I invite my mother who is in me to rejoice with me of the breath that enters, Exhaling I invite my mother who is in me to rejoice with me of the breath that goes out.

Breath in, feel relaxed...

breath out, feel calm...

Breath in, feel relaxed...

breath out, feel calm...

Breath in, feel relaxed...

breath out, feel calm...

Inhaling, I feel so light, Mom, you feel light as you are myself? Breathing in, I feel so free, Mother, do you feel free as I am?

My mother and I rejoice together to breathe together. My mother and I enjoy the exhalation together.

My father and I rejoice in the inspiration of my father, and I enjoy the exhalation together.

Breathing in, I see my heart like a flower.

Exhaling, I let my heart go open like a flower.

Breath in, feel relaxed...

breath out, feel calm...

Breath in, feel relaxed...

breath out, feel calm...

Breath in, feel relaxed...

breath out, feel calm...

Thank you.

Meditation for Drifting Off

You can follow through with this meditation after doing the previous one for becoming tired. You can also use it on its own in order to fall into a deep sleep. You will not be able to do anything after this, so make sure that you are only listening to this meditation as you are trying to fall asleep. You need to have enough time to doze off, too. This isn't for napping or only getting a couple of hours at night. This is for the individuals who are having trouble sleeping through the night.

Now that you are in a comfortable position, you are ready to start counting, which is a primary part of this deep-sleep, guided meditation. Ensure that you are in a relaxed space so that you can avoid shifting around too much.

The point of getting into a comfortable position is that you don't have the need to move around. Excessive moments while meditation will only cause you to go back into the beta state even if you may have already started to drift into the alpha state. And you don't want to go back into the beta mode as it entails that you will have another troubled night in bed. So, find that comfortable position and try to follow a breathing exercise.

Take in a deep breath, hold it in, and allow your stomach and chest to feel the tension that comes with the activity. When you exhale, you will feel more relaxed.

Then, start counting backward. You need to do a countdown. Start from ten and let the air release from your lungs. It is also important to count slowly so that you can push the tensed feeling out of your body.

In addition to counting, you have to do some visualizing as well. The visualization that we are talking about involves more than just imagining the numbers each time you are counting down. This is what you need to do in order to make this guided meditation more powerful.

Let's begin with the countdown once more. Allow your brain to become open to new ideas, and do not let your thoughts go anywhere towards reality. Do not think about work. Do not wonder about your relationships. Do not stray towards the thoughts of money, stress, food or anything else that constantly takes up your time. Focus only on letting your mind wander. Try to think freely. We will guide you, but you are the only one who can create the visuals in your head.

Start counting down now from ten. As you do this, you feel your breathing get slower in parts. 10...9...8...7...6...5...4...3...2...1.

Now, your breathing is much slower. You are able to feel the weight of the world rise above you and float away as you drift closer and closer to sleep. It is time to count down once again as you become more relaxed. 10...9...8...7...6...5...4...3...2...1. Your breathing is so slow that you are almost doing so as when you are asleep.

It is time to visualize yourself in a scenario that will help to guide you into a place where you are sleeping deeply. Start by allowing your mind to go black. We are going to count down once more. 10...9...8...7...6...5...4...3...2...1.

Your mind is blank. You do not see anything but darkness. Your eyes are closed, and there is nothing that you see. Eventually, a fuzzy image dissolves in your brain, and you begin to see a blank chalkboard in front of you.

As you look ahead, you notice that you are in a room with other people. You do not recognize them, and there is nothing striking about them. Everyone is wearing similarly plain clothing, all looking straight on quietly.

In front of the room is a very boring teacher. He is a middle-aged man, and his appearance or posture is not interesting either. You cannot hear what he is saying, but you can see that he is talking. You do not care about what he discusses, and he does not really seem to be that interested in his own words either.

You feel your eyes become heavier as you attempt to focus on this man ahead of you. Though you are struggling to stay awake, you are finding it difficult to remain alert. You try to pay attention to what he was saying, but it is nearly impossible as you feel yourself yawn.

The other students around you are just as quiet as well. The sun is shining through the window, but you can tell that it is starting to set. You only want to be home and stay in your bed, asleep. Instead, you are here, but it's okay because you won't be there for much longer.

As you look at the students who are surrounding you, you start to realize that they are drifting away one by one, too. You are not the only person who is having a hard time to keep your attention focused on whatever it is that the teacher in the classroom is trying to say.

You are feeling peaceful in this room, and it's clear that the others are feeling the same way. Though it is a time when your attention is needed, you start to let yourself indulge in the serenity of the place instead. No one is making a sound besides the man in front of the classroom, but you can still barely hear what he is talking about.

Your head is becoming heavier now, and all you want to do is let it hit the pillow. Your breathing gets slower, and you start to feel like it is easier to keep your eyes closed than open at this point.

Your lids are heavier than ever. Suddenly, you allow them to close. You open your eyes once more, but no one has noticed that you have begun to drift off.

You are now falling into a deep and heavy sleep.

For the remainder of this meditation, we are going to use verbal affirmations to help you go into a deep slumber. Allow yourself to no longer treat this as a recorded guide anymore; let these thoughts flow through your brain as if they are your own. They can help you drowse off effectively. These are the words that you should embody:

I am now asleep.

I am feeling my thoughts leave my brain. I am focused on resting peacefully.

I am allowed to fall into a heavy sleep.

I am safe and protected in my room. I deserve to be able to enjoy this luxury.

There is nothing for me to worry about.

No one is going to harm me as I sleep.

I can feel myself drifting away, deeper and deeper into a place that will help me feel more rested.

Being tired is not something that is going to cause me any more issues.

I am preparing myself in the best way I can now for whatever awaits me in the future.

The only thing that matters is that I am focused on falling asleep.

I am making sure that all of my attention is put on drifting away.

There is nothing I care about that will keep me awake at this point.

The most important thing at the moment is that I am fading into a deep sleep.

My body is completely relaxed.

I am now asleep.

As I count down from ten, I will be in an even deeper sleep and manage to stay asleep all night long.

10...9...8...7...6...5...4...3...2...1.

Meditate to Find Inner Peace and Stay Focused

This 5-minutes meditation is a commonly used method to clear your mind and be in the present moment. You can use this meditation technique to get rid of the negative energies that don't allow you to be vibrant and focused. The practice can make you experience a sense of protection from the negativity perceived to come from others. Research has shown that with regular practice, you should experience compassion and effortlessly detach your mind from troubles. Follow these simple steps:

1. Begin seated in a chair, preferably with the feet in contact with the ground, or instead sit on the floor in a cross-legged pose. Keep the spine tall.

2. Then close the eyes and continue to breathe in and out through the nostrils.

3. As you breathe, imagine that you are both physically or mentally letting go all the negative energies down the arms, torso and the legs.

4. Try to visualize that your entire body is surrounded by vibrant light or attractive color works.

5. Imagine that the light is to enter in the crown of the head and then is traveling down your entire body. Take time as you experience the light nourish your brain cells, heal the body organs and get to your fingers and toes.

6. Now bring your attention back to the bubble of light that surrounds the body. You should view the bubble as a protection that inhibits negative energies from reaching you.

7. Live the moment for 2-3 minutes to allow maximum penetration of the light or color works. Once your attention begins to fade, bring your attention back to the breathing patterns.

8. Wait until you feel ready to open your eyes, as meditation requires effortless transition from the conscious world to the real world.

Chapter 7.   Live a Mindful Life

Mini Habits Mindfulness Meditation

Anyone who wants to sail across the world would start with the first log to build a boat.

This is the same thinking that will be required for your long journey. This is not something that is going to cause you fear or stress. It is the way that you are going to get everything that you have ever hoped and dreamed for.

You are going to start now by focusing on your breathing. That is the most important thing you can do at any time. When you want to give in to a craving, when you want to skip the gym, or when you want to make any sort of decision that isn't in the best interest of your health, you are going to start by breathing.

Just breathe.

Feel the air pass through your body. You have your own air filtration system within your body.

You are powerful. You are starting to feel the tension leave your body. You're not holding onto any fear of this situation. You are excited to see what is waiting for you at the end of all your little battles.

This meditation is going to be a promise to yourself. You are going to promise to have mini habits in your daily life that will help bring you closer to achieving your goal.

You are going to promise yourself to do one healthy thing every single day, even when you feel like doing nothing at all.

As you start to let more healthy habits come into your life, it will become that much easier to see the positive transformation.

Continue to focus on your breathing now. This is the most powerful tool you will have throughout this journey.

Your healthy habits are going to start always with the air around you, and then with your mind. You are going to say "yes" when you know you should and stop avoiding things that are healthy for you.

You are going to fight through your biggest struggles. You are going to be brave for yourself. You are going to choose health for yourself.

You are promising your body that you will always be there to take care of it. You are grateful for the body that you have been given.

You are going to make a healthy choice to get the right amount of sleep each and every day.

You are going to make the healthy choice to go to bed at the right time and wake up before hitting snooze for the fifth time.

You are going to choose to eat a healthy breakfast and avoid anything that is too unhealthy for you.

You are going to choose to be kind to yourself even when you might make mistakes. You are going to choose to get right back to what you need to do even when you do something that could derail the process.

You are choosing to love yourself and make healthy habits a part of your life so that you can live as long as possible.

You are going to choose to move your body every single day. You are dedicated to moving even the slightest amount in order to get your heart pumping. You are not working out just to have an attractive body. You are already beautiful, and you know this. You are working out so that you can be healthy.

You feel the breath come in and out again. This is something that you will always have with you. You always have the ability to relax. You will always have the ability to find peace and serenity.

Finally, you will choose to stick to your keto and your fasting diet regimen. You will work with your body and make healthy decisions.

You feel yourself becoming more and more relaxed. You feel calm when you remember that you are making all of these healthy choices for your body. You feel the air as it continues to come in and out of your body. When we count down from ten, you will be able to drift asleep or move onto the next meditation.

Ten, nine, eight, seven, six, five, four, three, two, one.

Healthy Habits Affirmations

These affirmations are phrases that you should be saying to yourself as often as possible. You can write them down on pieces of paper and keep them around your home. You could have Post-it Notes on your mirror and fridge to keep you focused on the right things. Say at least ten affirmations every day. A good rule of thumb is five in the morning and five at night. State them more often if you can. Eventually, your brain will be rewired to think positively rather than negatively.

While listening to these affirmations, focus on your breathing. One good method to do this is to practice mental yoga at the same time. To do this, you will want to stand up straight, placing your pointer finger and thumb of your right hand on your left earlobe, and then your pointer finger and thumb of your left hand on your right earlobe. As you do this, you will have created an X across your chest.

Then, as we start to read, breathe in through your nose and out through your mouth. Slowly allow yourself to squat down into a squatting position, still holding your ears. Hold this position as we state one affirmation and then lift yourself back up. Repeat this process as needed in order to consistently listen to these healthy affirmations.

Another method you can do is to breathe in through your nose and out through your nose only. If you don't want to get up and do any mental yoga at the moment, you can simply do this nostril breathing exercise instead. You will want to take your right pinky and place it on your left nostril. Breathe in for three, and then take your right thumb and put it on your right nostril, releasing your pinky from the other nostril. Then, breathe out through this nostril. Repeat this process as you listen to these affirmations.

Practice this breathing method once before we get started. Breathe in through your right nostril for one, two, three, four, and five. Switch your thumb and pinky positions and breathe out for six, seven, eight, nine, and ten.

Fasting Affirmations

- I can do this.
- I do not need to eat right now.
- My body is healthy.
- I can feel my body losing weight.
- I feel myself become healthier and healthier as I fast.
- I do not need to listen to my stomach right now. I know what is best for my body.
- I find other ways to entertain myself.
- I am strong and powerful.
- I do not need food to make me happy.

- I do not need anything to make me happy. I am happy on my own.
- I am stronger than my biggest craving.
- Nothing is going to keep me from finishing this fast.
- No food is worth compromising my health.
- I am focused only on losing weight.
- I am centered around shedding pounds rapidly.
- I am not afraid to finish this fast.
- I do not give in to peer pressure to eat.
- I drink plenty of water every day.
- Fasting is easy.
- Fasting makes my body feel good.
- I know that these feelings of wanting to eat are only temporary.
- I deserve to have good health.
- I am doing this so that I live longer.
- I am doing this so that I feel better all the time.
- I will never give up.

Keto Affirmations

- My body knows exactly what to do.
- I understand my body and how to make it as healthy as possible.
- I am not afraid of my body's own processes.
- I am kind to my body.

- It feels good to eat a ketogenic diet.
- I can feel the fat burning as I diet.
- I give my body all the nourishment it needs.
- I focus only on making good decisions for my health.
- I am knowledgeable about my body.
- I am focused on losing more and more weight.
- I do not carry guilt about my past decisions.
- I feel my body healing from the decisions I used to make.
- I get closer to my goal of losing weight each and every day.
- I am connected to my body.
- My body is sacred, and I treat it this way.
- I am in control of my body. Food does not control me.
- I feel my mind becoming healthier as I continue to make healthy choices.
- I love the body that I have.
- My body is smart and keeps me safe.
- My body has brought me to exactly where I need to be.
- I am grateful for my struggles because they make me stronger.
- It feels so good to be so healthy.
- I feel health radiate through every part of my body.
- I do not let stress control me.
- I choose to make healthy decisions every day because it is exactly what my body needs and deserves.

Meditation for Healthier Habits

This meditation is going to be focused on forming healthier habits. Listen to this directly or repeat the script in your own voice and use that to help guide you through the meditation. Find a comfortable position and begin when you are ready. Let these thoughts flow through your mind naturally, as if you were saying them.

I can feel each breath that enters and exits my body. My breath comes in through my nose naturally. I don't even have to think about it and my body will breathe on its own. This is a habit that I developed before I even left my mother's womb. I breathe faster when I am nervous.

I breathe faster when I am excited. My breathing will slow as I become relaxed. When I am falling asleep, I can feel my breathing going incredibly slow. My breathing will regulate itself. This is a habit that I have, and it reminds me that I am human. When my breathing is happening in the snow, I can see it leave my body and make the air white. When I am breathing on a hot day, I can sometimes feel my own warm breath on my body, making me feel even hotter.

As I am breathing now, I am noticing this pattern. I am recognizing that habits are patterns that can come as naturally to me as breathing. Without even thinking about it, there are some habits that I participate in on a daily basis.

In the past, I have participated in habits that were not healthy, and that is OK. I wasn't always aware of the unhealthy habits that I had formed. There were things that took a little longer to realize were problems, and it wasn't something I was always able to do on my own either.

I am capable now of recognizing the unhealthy things that I have done in the past. These unhealthy habits included things like choosing a diet I knew wasn't healthy for my body or deciding not to exercise even though I knew I needed to get my body moving. I will not punish myself because of these unhealthy habits.

I am at peace with the choices I used to make for my body. Moving forward, I am going to focus only on forming habits that are healthy for me. I need to put an emphasis on doing things that are going to better my body, mind, and soul in the future, and not just now.

There is no better time to form a healthy habit then the moment I realize I need to include it in my lifestyle. The better I can get at recognizing and adding healthy habits, the easier it will be to change my life. I am aware of the things I need to start doing to better my life, and it is even easier to identify the things that I shouldn't do.

I will always be looking for new healthy habits to include in my life. I will remember that I need to continually check up on myself and ensure that I am making the right decisions for the right reasons.

There is nothing wrong with forming habits. I need to now focus on forming healthier ones that will help me for a longer period of time. Habits will take time to form. I am not going to be able to form all the habits I want overnight. I will make sure I try every single day to do something healthy.

From there, I will find the easiest habits to implement, and the ones that I need to alter to better fit into my life. I can form healthy habits, as long as I devote myself to making healthy choices every single day. Some healthy habits are going to form on their own. Others will need to be worked out over time.

This is completely natural. Easy habits for some people might be more challenging for me, and that is OK. I will go at my own pace, and the only thing that matters is that I will be devoted to adding these healthy habits into my life.

The more I put my attention on forming habits, the easier it will be to follow through with them. Habits will take as much time to break as they might have taken to form. It is OK to fall back into old habits, I just have to have the strength to pull me back out.

I will prepare for times when I might fall back into these habits so that I don't let it cause me too much disappointment. If I expect perfection throughout my habit-forming process, I will only set myself up to feel defeated. Instead, I will prepare with encouraging affirmations and positive thinking to help me through the times that I might feel like giving up.

Now it is time for me to enter the present world from this meditation and get focused on adding healthier habits to my life. I am going to put my mind towards ensuring that I am including meditation as one of my habits, as this will help improve my health as well. I start to exit this state of mind and return to a better, healthier place, more oriented on making healthy choices.

I can feel my breathing in a rhythmic pattern that helps to relax my mind, body, and soul. I breathe in again, remembering how it is like a pattern, a rhythm, a habit. I feel the breath leave my body, exhaling the bad habits, inhaling the good. As I exhale the bad habits, I keep remembering how I can start these good habits as soon as my breathing has regulated.

It is time to become either focused or drift asleep now. As I count down from ten again, I will be out of this meditative state and back into the world that will help me to form healthy habits successfully. Ten, nine, eight, seven, six, five, four, three, two, one.

5-Minute Quick Forces of Nature Meditation

This meditation can be practiced everywhere, as long as you can focus for 5 minutes. It's okay to meditate at the start of the day even while in bed, when seated on the floor or your car, at lunchtime break or in the evening as you relax after taking a nice bath. The key is to find a good timing and peaceful location where you can concentrate undisturbed for up to 5 minutes. Here is how to go about it:

-With eyes closed, start to focus on your breath. Ensure that you take slow but deep breaths in through the nose and out from the mouth.

-You should mentally set your mind to release all negative energy and the mind-inspired barrier with each breath you exhale. For the inhale, imagine that you're welcoming in calm and cool thoughts.

-Now visualize that you are lying down in the middle of a big and well-developed field during a sunny, cool day. Examine the vast field that extends all around you, and you can for now see the blossomed wildflowers and the blade of green grass.

-Try to feel the ground that is underneath you and let the gravity to pull your body weight deep and grounded to the surface.

-Then with more deep breaths, imagine a stream of liquid white light that is as bright as the sun, which pours down the clouds above and through the top of your head.

-Allow the white light to wash away those troublesome thoughts or the negative energy with each slow and steady breath. The liquid light should also fill each corner of your mind so that you can feel still, quiet and calmed down.

-Continue to breathe deeply and then visualize a gentle breeze that blows across your body organs. The breeze should also move the stream of liquid light down through the throat and deep into the heart.

-At this point, experience a pool of white light that fills up the heart; and gently wash any feelings of fear, anxiety, pain, anger and sadness. And as the bad memories get cleansed, your heart should glow with brilliant white light!

-Breath slowly as you visualize the light pooled in the heart start moving down the belly in order to release any tension accumulated there. The light should travel down the pelvis and break down the pains or negativities that could be making your hips tense.

-On the subsequent breath, let the flow of the white light to drop down into the base of the spine, as it sends spikes into various directions. The light should, at the last stage, extend down the legs and penetrate the soles of the feet.

-Likewise, the light should be able to carry all the negative feelings and cleanse the feet. With each breath, you should visualize the light carefully drain out of the body and quickly sink into the ground.

-At this point, visualize yourself standing up in the middle of the vast field and start to slowly walk with each step being lighter and more joyful. You should feel your body radiating with this liquid white light that fills each body organ, and extend a couple of feet in and out each direction you go.

-Believe that as you move through the remaining part of the day, the light will continue to radiate and positively influence people you come across with. The light should also shield you from the dark feelings or negative thoughts that may try to return.

The Eyes: Window into Wisdom

TIME: 10 TO 20 MINUTES

Western mindfulness meditation is generally done with the eyes closed. One of the main reasons for this is that, especially when first starting out, students need to minimize their distractions, and closing the eyes is an excellent way to reduce external stimulation. The main downside to this is that students may also become sleepy, floaty, or drift off to sleep with the eyes shut. When the eyes are "half open or half shut," external distractions are reduced, but there is still some orientation to the outside world. With the eyes open, one tends to remain more alert and oriented, though there is more possibility for external distractions. From a higher meditation perspective, however, it is said in Vajrayana that the eyes are the door and access to the higher Wisdom, and that we should learn to meditate with our eyes open. I have personally found this to be the case, and it also definitely prevents one from dozing off. Additionally, with eyes open, one can more fully integrate the meditative state into all aspects of life.

STEPS

1 Find a quiet place to sit, free from distractions. Using the same place in the beginning is often useful.

2 Sit with your spine straight but relaxed and eyes closed.

3 Breathe normally and settle in as you bring your attention to your breath at the nostrils.

4 Watch your breath, and notice it as you breathe in and out.

5 Do 5 minutes of meditation. Notice how you feel and any benefits or negative side effects of closing your eyes.

6 After 5 minutes, pause and rest for 1 minute, and then do 5 more minutes of meditation with your eyes half open. Pause and notice how you feel and any side effects.

7 Finally, sit with your eyes fully open for 5 minutes. As with the other two meditations, notice the benefits and difficulties, particularly in relation to the eyes being open.

8 You may wish to make some notes as to what you learned.

Guided Meditation

Meditation length: 30 minutes. I've noted places where you should pause and let the meditation continue in silence or with background music or ambient sounds. I have timed this out to be about 30 minutes, depending on the length of the pauses.

If you have a chime or a bell, it's a nice way to end the session.

Welcome and welcome yourself to this time of stress relief and relaxation.

Before we begin, I encourage you to stretch your arms and back as if you are having the first delicious yawn of the day. Really push your shoulders back and arms out. You may even yawn for real. Stretch as much as you can to help release some of the tension you may be bringing into this session with you. Move your spine forward and back so that it can relax into a position that is natural and comfortable for you. Don't push so hard that it hurts. This is when you start to listen to the knowledge your body has about itself. This feels good, but it also helps prepare your body for sitting in the meditation.

Pause one minute or two to allow the participants to complete the stretch and return to their position.

I invite you to take a position that is comfortable you. You may choose to sit or to lie down. It's important that you be comfortable in this position for about 30 minutes so you may want to sit with your back supported and feet flat on the ground, or have a pillow under your knees if you are lying down.

This meditation is for you, so don't feel that you have to meet anyone's expectations for how you sit. This is all about listening to your body and finding your path to relieve stress. Take the time to find your comfortable spot. You may find it useful to pause this while you get anything you might need to make you more comfortable. A blanket, a pillow, or anything else that is helpful.

Close your eyes lightly and become aware of how your body feels as you settle into the position you've chosen. Feel free at this time to move around a bit if you are uncomfortable. Wiggle on your sitting bones.

If you are sleepy, you may prefer to keep your eyes open. If so, lower them to a soft focus on the floor in front of you or on the ceiling if you are lying down.

Take a moment to feel the weight of your body on the chair and floor. Feel how you are supported without doing anything but being right here, right now.

Bring your attention to your breathing. Take three deep breathes at your own pace. Fill your lungs and abdomen as full as you can without raising your shoulders.

Notice where you are most aware of the breath. You may be most aware of how your abdomen rises and falls, or how the movement of air feels in your nose.

You may be aware of areas that feel tight when you try to inhale deeply. This is natural and it's ok. Sometimes, we are embarrassed to feel your stomachs get bigger as they fill with air.

Know that no one is watching. Be greedy. Breath is as much as you want.

Imagine the air is a golden light that fills your body. Your body knows how to use the air and knows how to use the light.

Be full of golden light!

Pause to let participants feel this image

Your mind will wander as you try to focus on your breathing. This is normal. It's what your mind is designed to do. Whenever you notice that your mind has wandered, take note of the distraction. You don't need to judge whether the distraction is good or bad. Just note that it is there, thank yourself for noticing, and bring your focus back to your breath.

Just focus on this breath. Feel it flowing into your body…

Now feel it flowing out.

All you have to think about is this one breath.

In

And out…

One at a time

In

And out...

You can repeat In... and out... a few times.

Shifting your focus from your breath, begin to scan your head and face for any areas of tension.

As we begin to scan the body, you may notice areas of tension. When you notice this, try to relax those muscles. You may find that a small stretch and release of the muscles helps reduce the tension. This doesn't have to be a big movement. It is something that resets the muscle memory into one of relaxation rather than tension.

Feel your forehead: Is it tight? Do you hold your worries there? If you notice tension, you may find that small movements will help you relax. Try raising your eyebrows and letting them fall back into place.

Feel for tension around your eyes. Maybe you are holding them too tightly closed. Imagine them relaxed and light.

Bring your attention to your cheeks and mouth. Relax your cheeks and bring the corners of your mouth slightly up into a kind of a private smile. It feels good to smile, doesn't it? It helps to relax the jaw and set the tongue lightly against the roof of your mouth.

Focus your attention on your neck. Does your head feel balanced? Tuck your chin slightly to lengthen the back of the neck. This will help to balance and release any tension.

Bring your awareness down to your shoulders which is where many people hold their stress. Raise and lower the shoulders a couple times. Move them on a circle if that is comfortable for you and let them relax into a neutral position. Feel their weight as they fall down and slightly away from the body.

Take a deep breath and feel your body fall into a relaxed position as your exhale.

Now feel your arms and hands. Rest your hands lightly on your legs (or the floor if you are lying down). Stretch the fingers just a bit to be sure you aren't holding tension there. Let your arms and hands be fully supported by your legs.

Moving your awareness around to your back feel for areas where your muscles are tight. Are you holding yourself up in a rigid position? Maybe you've arched your lower back so you are sitting up too straight. Relax into the chair or floor with your lower back flat.

Feel for tension if your hips and pelvis. You may find that a small twist in your lower back helps to release tension in the back and hips. Try making a small circle with your hips, like dancing on your chair.

Put your hand over your heart and feel for any tension in your chest. Take a few deep breaths and exhale whatever tension you feel there. Inhale slowly and really feel where the air is going.

It is normal to breathe less than we can. Right in this moment, you want to breathe as fully as possible.

Take another deep breath and feel your abdomen filling. Notice any ways that you stop the air. Maybe you are a bit nervous about what will happen if you really let go. This is normal Know that you are safe to breathe as deeply and fully and let go as much as you want in this safe environment. Relax your stomach muscles. No one is looking. Let it go.

Feel your legs. So important holding you up and grounding you to the earth. Notice any tension that you may be holding in our legs and relax. You won't fall over. Try stretching them in front of you and releasing them back with your feet flat on the floor. Point your toes into a good stretch and relax the leg fully.

Scan your body for any areas of tension that remain. Take note of those areas. They may be trying to tell you something but, right now, that can wait. Tell yourself that is ok to relax fully and just be here in this moment right now.

Feel what this state of full relaxation feels like. Maybe you haven't felt this relaxed in a while. Know that you can create this for yourself at any time.

 Take three deep breathes at your own pace. Linger a little longer on the exhale.

[this count is to give an idea of the speed of the breath. Take a few seconds for counting and then pause to let the participants catch up]

Inhale-1-2-3; exhale 1-2-3-4

Inhale 1-2-3; exhale 1-2-3-4

Inhale 1-2-3; exhale 1-2-3-4

Now let your breath return to its natural rhythm.

Pause for a few minutes to let the participants feel their natural breath

Let your body become heavy with relaxation and feel your weight as it presses against the chair (floor). You are being fully supported, not just by the chair where you are sitting, but by the whole earth beneath you. You don't have anything to do right now except feel your relaxed body being held and supported.

Take another deep breath and exhale slowly and then let your breathing return to its natural rate.

Continue to focus on your breath. Note any distractions that may come up and bring your mind back to your breathing. Don't worry about any stray thoughts. Everyone has them!

Count your breath [you may repeat the following a few times to set a rhythm]: inhale - 1..... exhale - 2.... inhale - 1.... exhale - 2....

Take each breath one at a time.

Focus on this breath. And this one

In

And out

In

And out

[continue this focus for a few minutes, to let the participants feel the meditation without narration. You can choose how long to let this go on]

Right now, you have nothing to do but be here in your body, supported by the whole earth and to breathe.

Take a deep breath and allow your breath to return its natural rate.

As you continue to breathe, note that, right now, in this moment, you have no worries. You are just a relaxed body. Any distractions that arise while you tell yourself this can wait.

Repeat the following phrases:

I am relaxed

I am balanced

I can deal with any worries later

I am relaxed

I am balanced

I can deal with any worries later

I am relaxed

I am balanced

I can deal with any worries later.

I am relaxed by focusing on my breath

I am balanced by being supported by the whole earth

I can deal with any worries later when I am ready for them

I am relaxed

I am balanced

I can deal with any worries later.

Continue to repeat these phrases to yourself silently for a few minutes.

Pause to allow the participants a few moments to repeat the phrases.

Know that, even if you have doubts, these things are true.

You are relaxed

You are balanced

You decide when to deal with your worries.

The whole earth supports you in your relaxation and balance. Feel yourself supported and held.

Feel that everything you have done in your life has brought you to this moment without errors or mistakes.

This moment is perfect.

When you feel doubt, say hello to it and let it know it can't distract you from your purpose.

You are relaxed

You are balanced

You can deal with all doubts and worries.

Pause a couple minutes to let the participants feel this.

Take three deep breaths and prepare to end this session.

Don't think of this as returning to the real world. You are bringing this feeling of relaxation back with you to become your real world.

Know that you can achieve this at any time because you are supported and held in balance.

Pause

Thank yourself for taking this time to connect with your body and balance.

Open your eyes and gently move your hands and feet.

  Before you get up, stretch your arms and back again, like a cat after a most satisfying nap. Stretch as much as you can. Feel yourself pushing your body into this world that is filled with all sorts of healing energy. Know that it is all there for you.

Part 3.   How to Manage Stress with Meditation

Chapter 8.   How to Manage Your Physical Stress

Stress, as we all know, is a contributing factor to a wide array of health concerns. The way society works these days it's hard not to feel overwhelmed now and then. Juggling family life, social life, a career, your finances, planning for the future, it's almost too easy to quickly feel burned out.

Stress and the Physical Effects on Your Body

No one is immune to stress. Everyone experiences it. The only difference is the way the symptoms affect you physically since everyone has their stress coping mechanisms. Some people have found ways to regulate their stress and keep it under control, while others quickly unravel and go off the deep end as soon as they begin to feel the first signs of stress. Not all stress is necessarily caused by external triggers alone. At times it could be attributed to a medical condition, which is something you can easily confirm by discussing these symptoms with your doctor.

The physical symptoms induced by stress include:

• Weight gain

• Insomnia

- Chronic fatigue

- Muscular aches

- Lower levels of energy resulting in lethargy

- Headaches or migraines

- Constipation, upset stomachs, diarrhea, nausea

- Rapid heartbeat which may cause chest pain

- Frequent illnesses, cold, and infection

- Loss of libido and poor sexual drive

- Physically shaking with anxiety

- Cold and sweaty palms and feet

- Dry mouth

- Jaw clenching

- Teeth grinding

- Difficulty swallowing

- Ringing in the ears for some people

These are just some of the many physical symptoms that are associated with excessive stress. Yet, we tend to brush it off and not think twice about the connection between these symptoms and stress. We're not aware of how constantly living in a state of stress is resulting in damaging effects on our health.

Stress is always going to be a part of life, so the way you learn to handle it is what truly matters. The best thing you could do for yourself physically is learning how to identify these stress symptoms and then making a conscious effort to be aware of its presence in your body. Never take these symptoms lightly because they could sometimes be indicative of other health problems. Should you be concerned that there might be something going on, don't hesitate to enlist the help of your doctor for a thorough evaluation.

Why Stressful Thoughts Are Damaging

Our thoughts can hurt us more than we know. When you add chronic stress on top of those negative thoughts, the physical and psychological effects can be profound. The problem with a negative mindset is that it acts like an anchor that weighs you down. At times, it may feel like you're drowning in your stress. There are warning signs to look out for that indicate your stress levels are threatening to get out of hand (if they haven't already), and something needs to change if you ever hope to learn how to manage your stress levels.

We know that stress is bad, but we rarely stop long enough to think of the reasons why. Continuing to live with such high levels of stress is purposely putting your entire wellbeing at risk. You're risking your emotional equilibrium, and you're risking your physical health unnecessarily. It's bad for your health, and it is even worse for your mind because:

• It Leaves You in A Constant State of Unhappiness - A negative mindset overshadowed by stress will blind you to all the good things you have going on in your life. No matter how much you have to be grateful for, you find yourself feeling unhappy and miserable all the time, which eventually strips you of any desire or ambition to grow and develop yourself. A prime example of how stress and negativity weigh you down like an anchor.

• You'll Continue to Be Haunted by Your Past - You find it hard to let go of the past, especially the mistakes and failures that you've faced. Mindfulness is about being present, but you can't do that if your past continues to linger on your mind. Emotional freedom becomes difficult and, at times, you might find yourself blaming other people or circumstances when you find yourself unable to accomplish a goal.

• All Your Mind Can Focus on Is Negativity - The more you dwell on your stress, the further into the black hole of despair you will seem to sink into. Staying positive daily becomes an immense challenge when stress meddles in the picture. Everything seems bleak and even the slightest things could trigger an emotional reaction from you. What's worse, you start to believe that will change and anything you do is just setting yourself up for another disappointment.

• You'll Be a Complainer - Since all you can focus on is everything that is causing you to stress out, complaints will begin to roll off your lips quicker than solutions will. You'll find yourself complaining about the same old thing repeatedly, yet doing very little in the way of finding a solution to the problem. If you find yourself doing this, it is high time you start changing your mindset for the better through mindfulness. No good will ever come out of complaining except to drive away the people who are close to you. Others will be quick to realize you're a complainer long before you come to that realization on your own. Would you want to be around someone who complains all the time?

• You'll Be Labelled a Pessimist - It goes hand in hand with being a complainer. When you lack the mental clarity to see the opportunities and possibilities for change, you begin to develop a pessimistic outlook. The only thing you'll be able to see are the reasons why it isn't going to work or succeed. You prefer to make excuses rather than make an actual effort to change and you find yourself being put-off by people who try to suggest doing things differently. There's always going to be a reason not to do something, the challenge now is to find reasons why you should do it instead.

• You're Stuck in A Constant State of Demotivation and Fatigue - You've lost count how many times you've uttered the phrase "I'm tired." It seems to be an everyday occurrence now.

Even when you wake up in the morning it feels like you're already tired. Not to mention feeling demoralized and a lack of desire to do anything, even if it is something as small as meeting a couple of friends for dinner. How many times have you found yourself guilty of bailing out on plans and canceling activities because you "didn't feel like it?" If your answer is far too often or more than you would have liked, that's another example of just how damaging stressful thoughts can be. If you find yourself lacking a zest for life, it's a sure sign that something needs to change and quick.

• Self-Criticism Becomes Second Nature - Chronic stress is going to blind you to your true potential and capabilities. All your flaws seem larger than life when you're stressed. Even when others compliment you on a job well done, you'll find a way to downplay those compliments and replace them with self-criticism instead. Everyone has the power within them to change for the better, more power than they realize. Except that it's hard to see all that when your stress has taken control over your life. Until you change your mindset and learn to regulate your stress, you'll never appreciate the precious moments happening in front of you until it's too late and the moment has gone.

• It Encourages the "Victim" Mentality - A clear sign that it is time to change your mindset is when you see yourself as a victim of your circumstances or situation. Why me, this always happens to me, are all too common phrases you'll hear from the chronically stressed. Believing you're a victim is a result of having low self-esteem, another byproduct of being stressed. The only way to change this is through mindfulness. It may not be easy, but it is going to be one of the most life-changing decisions you make.

Managing Physical Stress in Everyday Life

Learning how to manage your stress takes patience and practice. Your body needs to heal for the sake of your wellbeing. You and you alone must take the time to take care of your body before it eventually starts to give up on you. Find the time to do it because your health depends on it.

• Sweat It Out - Physical exercise is the best relaxation technique out there for both your mind and body that won't cost you a thing. Your lifestyle habits play a big part in the current state of your stress levels. It is recommended that you exercise at least three to four times a week for 30-minutes per session. Perform moderate to intense exercises like jogging, brisk walking, cycling, hiking, or any form of aerobic activity that is going to get your heart rate up. This gives your endorphin levels a boost, a hormone that helps you feel good and feel happy. The perfect antidote to combat stress.

• Stretch Frequently - Each time you come to the mindful realization that you're feeling stressed, stand up and stretch. Roll your shoulders, roll your neck, stretch out your arms in front of you, walk around to loosen up your body. Schedule a massage session into work on those areas of your body you can't reach by yourself.

• Minimizing Intake - In this case, it refers to minimizing your intake of alcohol, caffeine, and nicotine. If you can't avoid it entirely, at least work on reducing your intake. Nicotine and caffeine are well-known stimulants that aggravate stress levels. Meanwhile, alcohol may act as a depressant when it is consumed in large quantities, but in smaller doses, it becomes a stimulant for stress instead. Therefore, trying to alleviate your stress with either of these options could end up aggravating it instead. Opt for water, fruit juices or herbal teas instead. The latter has been known to have a calming effect on the brain and body. A well-balanced and nutritious diet is always the best solution.

• Sleep, You Need It - Sleep is when your body works on repairing itself on the inside, and each time you deprive yourself of the necessary sleep hours, you're inadvertently contributing to your stress. Unfortunately, sometimes chronic stress has a nasty habit of disrupting our sleep patterns, making it difficult to get the deep, relaxing sleep that we need. Instead of relying on medication to induce sleep, an even better option is to try as many relaxation techniques as you've got time for before you head to bed. Even better, turn your bedroom into an environment that is warm, soothing, and relaxing with little to no disruptions at all. Your room should be nothing but a tranquil, serene oasis. Nothing that is going to remind you of your stress should be present in your room. Meditate, relax, unwind, or do any activity that relaxes you at least an hour before bed to give your brain the time it needs to start winding down. It is also important to try and set a bedtime routine and aim to sleep at about the same time daily, so your body gets adjusted to this routine.

• Warm Compress - Wrap a warm compress around your neck and shoulder area anywhere from 10-15 minutes or until the compress starts to lose its heat. As you do this, close your eyes, and allow yourself to relax as you feel the heat soothe your muscles. Place the warm compress on any area you feel tense or muscle tightness.

• Stop When You Feel Unwell - Don't force yourself to keep going if you genuinely feel unwell. This is your body's way of telling you that you need to slow down before your health gets worse. Pushing ahead when you can't focus or feel ill is going to compromise the quality of your work regardless. You may be able to finish, but you might not have done a good job on the task the way you otherwise would have. Stop and listen to what your body is telling you.

It's Time to Reduce Those Stressful Thoughts

You may not be able to get rid of them entirely, but you can learn to minimize the occurrence of these stressful thoughts.

That's the aim of mindfulness for stress management. To help you better manage your stress before it escalates into more serious conditions.

• Talking About It - Having someone you trust to talk about your feelings with can feel good. Open the door to all those feelings you've been holding inside and let it burst forth. Talking about it out loud is a way of channeling your stress externally so the tension is not built-up inside you. It can be a helpful exercise in reducing the stressful thoughts you have since talking things over helps you see things in a different light. Sometimes the person you're talking too could put things into perspective and give you the clarity you need to find a workable solution to your problem.

• Keeping A Diary - The way you might have done when you were a kid, except this time, the diary is for your stress. A stress diary if you will. It's another effective stress management tool that works on several levels. One, it's a way for you to channel your feelings and pour your stress out without hurting anyone or yourself. Two, it encourages mindfulness when you have to think about what you're writing. Three, it's an exercise in reflection that allows you to analyze the stressful episodes you had, when it happened, why it happened, how it happened and the way that you handled it. It gives you the opportunity to think about what you would do better should you be faced with the same situation again.

• No Negative Dialogue - Do not give into it and whenever you catch yourself in a negative thought, stop immediately because you are only going to make yourself feel worse. You're going to have to rely on mindfulness to make an active effort at turning your thoughts around into something positive. Look at what you've written in your diary and see how many of those thoughts that you penned down are negative. By being mindful of the thoughts that creep into your head, you're instantly more attuned to what those thoughts are and how they make you feel. If it is bad for you or going to affect your confidence levels, you need to put a stop to it immediately. This is going to require some practice but it can be done.

• Celebrate Your Little Victories - Even if they are small accomplishments. It may not feel like much, but its effectiveness lies in giving you something else to focus on other than your stressful thoughts. An accomplishment is still a victory, regardless of its size. You did something incredible and you should be proud of it. It wouldn't be called an accomplishment if it was easy, and it is time to make celebrating successes a habit. If you put in the effort and you reached a goal that you set out to do, feel proud and remind yourself of just how capable you are. Celebrate the success, feel triumphant and, more importantly, feel good about yourself.

• Distancing Cognitively - If you carefully examined the stressful thoughts you had, most of them would be based on worries that are not always entirely true. Stress has a way of blowing things out of proportion, speculating, and adding on what we believe may be facts, but they aren't. Most of the time, these worst-case scenarios are unlikely to happen at all. Think about all the worst-case scenarios you've stressed over the past. How many of them turned out to be true? To reduce the impact these thoughts have on you, balance your tendency to fall back on the worst-case scenario by replacing it with an optimistic thought or prediction. Instead of thinking "What if this fails miserably?" replace that thought with "Think of all the other possibilities when this succeeds!"

• You Have to Say No - You may not want to do it. You may feel bad about it. But you need to do it for the sake of your stress management. You know that having too much to do and too little time to do it is going to cause a great deal of stress to you, yet you still find yourself saying "yes" because you feel guilty or pressured into doing so. Worrying about missed opportunities, feeling conflicted, and the fear of being rejected is going to hold you back from saying no. If you hope to learn how to manage and reduce your stressful thoughts though, this is something you're going to have to start getting comfortable with.

• Adapt and Accept, Avoid and Alter - Stress can be triggered by any number of things. Some predictable, and others you don't see coming. Each stressful thought is an opportunity for things to get out of control unless you reduce these thoughts by adapting and accepting, avoiding, and altering. Adapt to the circumstances and work with what you've got. Accept that some things are beyond your control. Avoid getting worked up about it if it's not going to change anything. Alter your routine or plan of action if it will help make the situation better.

• Connect with Love - There's nothing that reminds you of how much you have to be grateful for quite like connecting with the people you love. The people who love you in return. The ones who make you feel safe, secure, and understood. Connecting with your loved ones is a natural stress reliever for both the mind and body. They may not be able to fix your stress entirely, but being in their company, talking about something else other than your worries, maybe even laughing and having a good time, can wash away all the unpleasant thoughts you were struggling to shake.

• Find A De-Stressor That Works - Everyone has got something that they find soothing and relaxing. It could be reading a good book, going for a hike to be one with nature, listening to soft, mellow music, spending time around your pet, going to the gym, catching up with friends, watching your favorite program on Netflix. Everyone has at least one activity that helps them feel better, and it's time to start tapping into it as often as you need.

Chapter 9. How to Manage Your Mental Stress

Free Ourselves from The Hands of Stress

No matter how many lists of practical tips and motivation I provide you with throughout this book, if you really want to get rid of stress for good, you'll need to get to the cause of it eventually. We all need to dig a little deeper if we want to truly free ourselves from the hands of stress. For most of us, there isn't going to be just one single thing at the root of the problem, but rather many things of varying importance and magnitude. It can be hard to see through the fog. It can be hard to understand why we feel the way we do. It is frustrating when we get stressed out about little things; we may get angry at ourselves for getting worked up over nothing or we might worry that there is something more sinister at work. And yes, sometimes there is something bigger going on, like depression, and if that is the case, it will obviously need to be addressed. Depression and stress have been known to go hand in hand. Stress itself can cause things like depression and mood swings, and depression can cause stress. However, it would be naive to assume that stress is merely a mask for depression for everyone. We all experience stress, regardless of our mental health. But if you're committed to getting rid of stress for good, you might need to do some self-exploration in order to get to the bottom of it. There are countless things that could be causing your stress levels to rise or hang around longer than you'd like. In this section, I will narrow these things down to a few common causes of stress that most of us face throughout life. There should be a number of relevant ideas here for every reader to benefit from.

In today's world, most of our lives are fast paced, and it can be hard to find a sense of inner peace when we're surrounded by chaos. For whatever reason, most of us are constantly busy these days. Some of us are workaholics, others like the buzz we get from adrenaline, and plenty of us simply have no choice in the matter. You already know from reading up to this point that being contactable at all times doesn't help stress. You know that having no structure in your life and staring at screens all day prevents your mind from achieving a stable foundation. It makes you tired and impatient. But what about the chaos that's out of your control? What about your racing thoughts or general restlessness? What about the times you forget things or struggle to concentrate?

We can start tackling these things by slowing everything down and taking one thing at a time. Remember that racing thoughts and self-doubt are big contributors where stress is concerned, so think about some ways you can cut through them. When you can't get a hold on your thoughts, close your eyes and do some 5/7 breathing. Train your brain to silence the things you have no control over and the things that are currently in limbo. Practice this every day. As soon as you hear yourself worrying or stressing out about things that are out of your hands, recognize it and stop it. Tell yourself that your brain energy could be put to better use. Focus on doing one task at a time when your mind is in this type of flurry. Multitasking is great when you're in good form but it doesn't help when your head is spinning. Remember to slow your physical movements down as well. Get perspective on the matter and ask for help wherever possible. Even when things seem to be of extreme importance today, ask yourself how much they will matter in the long run.

- What will happen if things don't get done the way you'd like them to today?
- Will it create a long-term problem or a short-term problem?
- Will anyone get hurt?
- Will you be able to recover, even if that means having to put in a little extra work?

When we take the time to ask ourselves questions like this, we are actively taking ourselves off the stress cliff. Self-reflection can be a lifesaving habit if you practice it enough. Being able to slow down your thoughts and bring yourself back down to earth is a skill that all of us can benefit from, so keep at it. Keep practicing.

Remember that organization is a total stress buster because it brings order to the things that are stressing us out. So when things are particularly hectic, try to keep all the things you're in charge of well organized. If you're in a heightened state, you might benefit from taking a half hour to write some lists or rearrange your schedule for the week. It could be time well spent. Once you've slowed down your thinking and gotten yourself organized, do your absolute best to keep your stress compartmentalized. By this I mean to keep work at work and home at home. Try not to bring work stress into the household, and when times are tough on a personal level, do your best to shield yourself from it when you need to be productive at work. Don't stomach the stress so it'll rear its ugly head later, just set it to one side when it's time to focus on other things.

One thing I'd like to discuss here is something called imposter syndrome. Whether you've heard of it or not, this is something that most people will feel at one point or another in their lives. It may strike when you're feeling low or when things are particularly stressful, but other times it can come out of nowhere. You might have it all the time or it may come and go. Put simply, imposter syndrome is an intrusive thought that makes you believe you're a fraud, despite any evidence working against that theory. It is usually accompanied by a fear of being "found out" or exposed. It can range from fleeting moments of self-doubt to full blown negative self-beliefs despite one's intelligence, success, or any other evidence of being an entirely competent individual. Imposter syndrome can affect just about anyone, but more often than not, it is experienced by people who have achieved highly in life or who have high-powered careers. It feels as though you don't deserve to be where you are in life or as though you've been faking it the whole time.

Another common facet of imposter syndrome is an inability to recognize when you've done something worthy of praise or reward. You may put things down to luck or consider it a fluke when things go your way, even if you've put a lot of hard work and expertise into the project at hand. You'll either experience these moments spontaneously and sporadically, or you might chronically feel as though you're faking your way through life and someone could "figure you out" at any time. But imposter syndrome isn't your brain telling you that you're actually faking. It's just flagging up something deeper, like self-doubt, uncertainty, guilt, high stress levels, or anxiety regarding future success. If you ask a bunch of your friends if they've ever felt this way, chances are most or all of them will have experienced this at some point, and knowing that can be quite comforting. But if we take the time to look at imposter syndrome more deeply, if we really dig into it, we'll usually find just a few things at the foundation, and they are: a fear of rejection, a need for approval, and/or feelings of inadequacy. Rejection, approval, and inadequacy can be seriously stressful tormenters. We all need to be approved of. No matter how strong our exterior is, knowing that someone appreciates you, respects you, and looks up to you is food for the soul. It's the thing that makes us stop feeling like imposters and gives us a chance to fully own our successes. We all require validation in order to carry on doing what we're doing and if we don't get that, it's only natural that we will begin to doubt our abilities and purpose in life. Our need for approval begins in childhood and stays with us for most of our lives. It's an important building block to our self-esteem, our identity, and our feelings of belonging within society. Without sufficient approval from others, we can develop feelings of being different, out casted, or simply not good enough.

Rejection shares many similarities with the absence of approval. It can pull the rug right out from under your feet no matter how strong you felt beforehand. It too, can make us doubt ourselves and our capabilities. It can make us feel shame and embarrassment, even when we have no real reason to feel that way. It can wreak havoc on our self-esteem. The thing about rejection is that it's quite a broad subject when you think about it. We don't just reel rejected when we're not chosen to be someone's companion. We feel rejection when we've worked hard at something and fail to get recognition for it. We feel rejection when we create something that people respond negatively or indifferently too. We feel rejection when people don't notice changes that we've made in our lives. And of course, we feel rejection when we really care about something and the people in our lives are unsupportive of it. Feelings of rejection can torment the mind.

In addition to the pain of rejection, feeling inadequate can also have detrimental effects on our self-image and confidence. It holds us back from taking risks. It makes us feel like we don't belong to be where we are; that everyone else is better or more worthy than us and that we have no place among our peers. We might become bitter or resentful of the people who surpass us in life. We might become jealous or disappointed in ourselves. And we're likely to find it hard to progress in life for fear of failure. As I'm sure you know or can imagine, these feelings are toxic. They feed imposter syndrome and stress, so you have to break free from them.

The Secret Beast We Must Slay

Here are three ways you can smash through your imposter syndrome and keep your head in the game:

1 - Stop trying to keep up with the Joneses.

You have to stop comparing yourself to others. You must be able to judge yourself by your own criteria rather than judging yourself based on the successes and lives of others. Your values and desires do not have to match everyone else's. What matters is that you allow yourself to appreciate the things that you like about your life. There may be things about you or your life that don't live up to other people's standards. But if those things are enough for you, that's all that matters. Look at your past as the background of your current life.

- How did you get where you are today?
- Did you overcome obstacles?
- Have you survived hard times?
- Don't you deserve credit for getting this far?

We have to be able to approve of ourselves if we're ever going to get anywhere in life. This can be hard for people who have had difficult pasts. If you feel as though one or both of your parents never approved of you as a child, you're likely to find it hard to approve of yourself in adulthood. If you've always come in second place, you're probably in need of a self-esteem boost. But you have to be able to do that for yourself. You have to be able to look at your accomplishments with pride. Every time you have overcome an obstacle in life, you have proven to yourself that you are worthy of praise and approval. Focus on your achievements and hold onto them when imposter syndrome tries to knock you down. Do something nice for yourself when you've risen to a challenge. It doesn't matter how big or small your accomplishments are. You may have simply gotten through a tough day. But being able to recognize that and reward yourself means that you are actively approving of yourself. You are changing any bad habits that could be causing you to experience imposter syndrome or stress. Practice doing this and commit yourself to making it a habit because it's one that will serve you well in life.

Being able to approve of yourself can lift you up after a fall and prop you up on days you're not at your best. Practice by reflecting on your accomplishments each day. Force yourself to end the day by writing down three or more things that you have done well today. It may seem like a frivolous exercise but doing this gives you an opportunity to pat yourself on the back. We need to be able to encourage ourselves, not just doubt ourselves or put ourselves down. Self-approval can be the hardest approval to gain, but when we have it, so many of our fears disappear.

2 - Look at the evidence.

When you're caught up in negative thought cycles brought on by imposter syndrome, it's easy to think that you don't belong where you are. It's easy to get lost in thoughts of inadequacy. Negative thoughts are a part of life but they're not the easiest things to tame. Sometimes you need a weapon to cut through them, and that's where evidence comes in. When you get the fear, take a moment to think about why you are where you are.

- How did you get here?
- Has your life experience helped you to get to this point in life?
- What have you done in the past that might help prove to yourself that you're good enough?

- What skills, knowledge, and expertise do you have?
- Are there things you can do better than anyone else can?

Look at how you got to this moment and big yourself up. Whether you studied for years at university or you made something out of nothing, there is a reason you have the things you do.

- You have overcome difficulties in the past; this means you are resilient.
- You have stuck with things to the end; this means you are dedicated.

You have learned and grown throughout your life. That means that you can continue to do so. Talk yourself off that ledge by looking at your accomplishments through positive, honest eyes, not doubtful ones. Let the evidence show that you deserve the good things in your life. Take ownership and pride in that thought.

3 - Rise up!

In life, we have to be able to use our negative emotions as fuel. If you feel inadequate today, do something to prove that you're not. If you feel like you don't approve of yourself right now, do something that will harvest that approval. Fix something that didn't go as you planned. Challenge yourself. Face a fear. If you're afraid of failing, take a risk. We do not get enough time on this earth to waste it all on self-doubt. There is no time for self-pity or self-loathing. There is only time to get better and do better. Take your negative feelings and all your fear and turn them into fire. Be the person you want to be. Be the person that you can approve of. Because why be anything else?

The next thing you might want to consider as a potential background of your stress is a certain type of addiction. I'm not talking about alcohol or substance abuse, but rather I'm suggesting that those of us with addictive personalities can become addicted to specific feelings. When you're thinking about stress and what lies beneath it, is it possible that you could be addicted to adrenalin? We've all heard the phrase "adrenalin junkie" and usually it's used regarding people who enjoy extreme sports and adventure. But leaping from a plane isn't the only way to get your heart pounding. Being late to a meeting can actually do the same thing. It is very possible that people who are perpetually late to work or other obligations are living in a state of adrenalin buzz. Because rushing around with the fear of being late kicks us into overdrive. Someone with habits like this is likely to find it hard to relax. They might pace around the house a lot, cleaning and fixing things rather than sitting down and taking a break. They might be constantly rushing around, trying to do too much at once, and unable to get their feet back on solid ground.

When we're high on adrenalin, our minds and bodies are naturally going to be in heightened states. Adrenalin gets us worked up. We can't concentrate or slow our thinking down. We can't focus on one task because we're too activated. We might feel anxious or impatient. Most importantly, when we're in this state, our stress levels could be through the roof. If you're addicted to adrenalin, you might be in that heightened state a lot. You might not take sufficient time to wind down and relax. You might feel constantly on edge. Take some time to think about your own behavior and habits.

Do you feel like you're constantly on the go?

Are you often worked up or do you feel like you're "buzzing" a lot?

Do you think adrenalin plays a role in your stress?

If so, you might want to consider some relaxation exercises such as yoga or meditation. You might benefit from using some lavender oil on your pulse points or in a diffuser in your home. Lavender oil is great when it comes to getting your body and mind to slow down and relax. Taking substantial time away from screens will also help to steady your mind and bring you back to earth. As I have said, again and again, you should aim to have screen-free time and quiet time every single day. Your body and mind need a chance to recover from the adrenalin coursing through your veins. If you are often running late, spend the next couple of weeks getting rid of that habit. Running around like a headless chicken isn't good for anybody, especially where stress is concerned.

Chapter 10. How to Control Your Thoughts

We are now going to discuss perception, so sit back and think about what you consider may be stressful things that happen on a daily basis. Things like; your boss getting on your nerves, you failed a test, you were late to school or whatever it is that you think causes your feelings of stress or anxiety.

Someone else may look at these events as a challenge. Others may look at it as just part of everyday life, while some people just look at it as things that happen and nothing serious at all.

It is all about perception and how you perceive these things. The first thing you can do in controlling your thoughts changes the way you perceive everything, and most situations do not have to be as stressful as we tend to make them.

Most of the time they are not; it is your perception of what is happening that is stressing you out, so learn to change how you see things and change your perception of everything that you go through.

You will begin to see that this will automatically reduce the amount of stress that you think you feel because most of the time, it is not even that serious.

Schedule Time to Worry

Are you one of those people that just cannot stop worrying no matter what? You can read a thousand self-help books, watch videos, listen to self-help DVDs and even attend conferences, but you just have one of those personalities that worry constantly.

Well, that is okay because we have a cool way that you can deal with that. We all know somebody who we have told a thousand times to stop worrying, and we have all probably been in situations where people have told us to stop worrying. That is just not a reality for certain people. The bottom line is that certain people are going to worry all of the time.

Especially those who are addicted to worrying, so we came up with ways to deal with those of you who are constant worriers. We always talk about living in your truth, changing what you can, and dealing with what you cannot. About being able to focus on working through those things that you cannot change and trying to be better.

You should take fifteen minutes every day and schedule this time so you can sit and worry about everything you need to worry about. All of your problems, your friends' problems, your job, the children, and whatever it is that you worry about constantly.

You're going to use this time as you're 'worry time' and schedule it each and every day. No matter what, this is going to become an important part of your daily life. It is just like when we talked about the importance of scheduling your morning stretches, your prayers, exercise, and your meditations. Now it is time to schedule your time to worry as well.

Five to ten minutes of me-time every day, at least once a day, preferably twice. Time when you can worry!! If you happen to be one of those worrywarts, this will probably be very relaxing for you.

Worrying is part of being who you are. You are aware of it and have now scheduled a time to get it done each day. Now that is it for the rest of the day. Now you can focus on your life and get through your day living a productive, effective lifestyle.

Once again, you're going to schedule as worry time fifteen minutes every day, get your worry on and get it out of your system. I do not understand people that like to worry constantly, but certain people actually feel the need to always be worried about something.

And if you have this kind of personality, I am sure that you will be able to find something to worry about if there's nothing present you will create something. Because most of the time, that is what you are doing anyway, creating something to worry about if you don't have anything there.

It is such a habit for you, so now we are going to schedule a time for you to do it daily without judgment or interruption. Sit and do nothing but worry, and that way, it will be so that you can get it all out of your system.

Now you can manage to get through your day without stressing yourself out with all this excessive and extra worrying because you take time and get it out the way each and every morning.

Breathing

Breathing is a requirement of life, it just happens, and we do not pay much attention to it unless something happens, which makes us need to pay attention to it. We may be choking, drowning, or we can be experiencing a bad cold. That is when we focus on the fact that we are having a hard time breathing or that we cannot breathe at all. Once again, we only pay attention when something happens.

During meditation, you force yourself to pay attention to your breathing and to be aware of it, which usually changes all of the time, depending on what your mind and body are doing at that time.

You can feel your breath, and in the next moment, you forget it because something else has entered your mind. Learn to keep your mind settled while you get in touch with your breathing for a few moments.

It takes extreme attentiveness to focus on your breathing when your attention is so easily pulled in other places. The same way sounds never stop hitting our ears sites never stop hitting our eyes or breaths never stops coming in and out of our bodies as long as we are living.

Each and every second of every moment, we are always somewhere in the cycle of breathing. So, when we practice, no matter what we're doing, we are giving ourselves over to the sensations throughout the body that are associated with the breathing that is going on, regardless of whether we connect with it or not.

Now that we are purposely mindful of your breathing, tune into each of those breath sensations gently, allowing our tensions to be focused on each breath.

Actually, you can take yourself away from thinking about the breath and actually feel the sensation while breathing like you are riding away from an ocean. Each time you breathe, you are going up and down on the wave.

Whether we are sitting still relaxing moving through our day or working, we can still be aware of our breath movement. Mindfulness is the quality of awareness, the core property of the mind itself, and it gets strengthened by sustaining our influence in the field of knowledge.

But the act of knowing is called wisdom, and it comes from trusting your original mind. The more we practice aiming and sustaining our attention on something, the more we learn to rest effortlessly.

Relax

Have you ever taken a hot bubble bath with the lights off and have nothing but candles burning? Mind you; they are aromatherapy candles burning. If you do not have a candle, use a strong scented bubble bath, it can be very relaxing.

Sit there and enjoy your relaxation for at least an hour and just really lose yourself. It will do something great to your spirit as well, so it makes you feel good inside and out.

Having common relaxing music playing, especially if it is playing really low and there is no other noise around, this can increase the level of relaxation that you will feel and experience.

Prepare for Stress

If you are blessed enough to have advance knowledge of something that will probably cause you stress, then you have a chance to mentally prepare yourself for what is to come.

The more you know about a stressful situation, like when it is and how long it may last, the more you can figure out what to expect, which automatically lowers the level of stress that that situation will cause you.

Making Sure to Stay Healthy

This is going to involve drinking more water and simple things that we hear all of the time but that we just never do. But they are very easy to do as well as very important for living a healthy life.

Avoiding too much alcohol, exercising daily, meditating, eating healthily, and getting enough sleep are a few easy things that can immediately be added to your schedule. Waking up just fifteen minutes earlier every day to make sure you stretch, you will be amazed at how it makes your body feel.

Remember not to drink too much. You really should not be drinking at all, but if you do, just remember not to drink too much. Alcohol is never good for your body at any time, in any way, and it is known to enhance or cause depression.

Try your best to meditate when you can practice any type of form of relaxation that you can, keep journals, and write down the way you think and feel every day. Repeat all of those positive affirmations to yourself daily. These are just a few simple things that can just improve your existence on the planet as a human being.

The more you exercise on a regular basis, the more your body will repay you or reciprocate you and love you for it. Your body loves exercise, and it can only help as it ages, grows and matures. So once again, when you exercise, your body will pay you back with positive benefits.

Eventually, it is going to assist you with getting rid of all that stress, depression, and anxiety. Those bones feel intense, and your muscles are all scrunched up and tense, all that is going to go away with regular stretching and exercise.

You are just going to feel better physically getting through your day without having all those knots all over your body, by doing a simple ten minutes of stretching every day and figuring out how to exercise a couple of days every week.

There a few other simple things and terms of trying to live a healthier life. You can eat a variety of foods, more fruits and vegetables, and incorporate more whole foods into your diet.

That's not to say that you need to completely change the way you eat, just increase the amount of vegetables and the variety of different foods. I would say get rid of caffeine altogether, but if you cannot, at least try to minimize the amount of caffeine that you take into your body.

The more water you are drinking, the more exercise your body is getting, it is not going to respond to that caffeine in the same way it used to. So, this should make it just a little easier for you to cut back on it or let it go completely.

You can also start taking your vitamins every day. A multivitamin works really well. Unless you know you have certain deficiencies, then you want to make sure you take those specific vitamins. Some people have serious vitamin D deficiencies if they do not get enough sun, so they take the supplements.

Just make sure you are taking your vitamin D on a regular basis. If you do not have a known deficiency that you are aware of, then just take them multivitamins and just get used to being aware that your body needs its vitamins and minerals each day. There are plenty of different ways to get it, but the multivitamin is a very simple and easy way.

Opposite

Get out of your regular routine of how you do things every day, even the way you live your life should get a few changes as well. It is time to change everything that makes you comfortable and do something totally opposite to that.

If you usually walk slowly, change your pace and try to walk fast for a week or two. Walmart is a place that many people shop at, if you are one of them, shop at Target for the next few weeks. How about changing the place where you get your gas for a week?

Anything that will take you out of your comfort zone and force you to try something that makes you feel a little uneasy, that is what you want to experience. And once you try this exercise, make it a regular habit.

Start to do it weekly, changing your daily routine, doing something different during your lunch break at work, or even going out and getting a bold new haircut! This will help you to become more open, welcoming, and embrace change, and you will be excited about new challenges.

Because you have forced yourself to try new and different things, you now welcome changes and embrace challenges in your life. As a matter of fact, you look forward to new possibilities because you have got used to being challenged.

You have embraced it, and now you wait for it, and if it takes too long to come, you are going to go out and look for it again.

Then you will automatically seek new and creative ways to test yourself. Now that is a good sign of being proactive and prepared. As humans, we always operate on the side that is most comfortable for us, and now it is time to use that opposite side, make yourself uncomfortable and make a habit of doing so daily so that you can constantly and purposely challenge yourself.

Isolation

Another huge cause for stress is not having emotional support and loving people around you when you feel stressed out or depressed or even anxious. You tend to isolate yourself from others and prefer being alone, but that is not good for you at all, because with you already being stressed, it will add more negative emotions.

When you are dealing with a high level of stress, isolating yourself from others can actually increase the stress level, create anxiety and depression, and take away from your self-confidence and your self-esteem.

If you do not already have friends, it will be in your best interest to at least try to make a few friends. Please do not fear making new friends because some may have hurt you in the past or may have dealt with trust issues, never fear starting new friendships or falling in love again.

Have the courage to love again, and always one more time!! The same goes for relationships that do not involve a loving partnership. We want to be open and willing to start new friendships at all times. This is the way we learn and grow in life by being around interacting with other people.

You can honestly be in danger of becoming even more isolated, more stressed, more depressed, and finally, dependent on being alone in being with other people. And eventually, you will become detached from reality and what is really going on out in the real world, and it will be harder to get yourself out of the habit of isolating yourself.

The longer you allow yourself to be detached from the world, then the more you start to feel trapped, helpless, and hopeless. You are going to feel like it is impossible to change and that nothing can be done to make your life become better or more positive, and you are going to fall deeper and deeper into that trap each day so that you keep yourself isolated from the rest of the world.

And like we have stated in this book many times, you become what you believe, so the more you believe you cannot get out of that position, then the longer you will stay in that situation.

The more you believe that you are so stressed that no one is able to help you, the more your mind is going be convinced of that negative fact. Over and over, you have told your body and your spirit that this is just how your life is, and there is no changing it.

You now are falling deeper and deeper into the trap of feeling like your life is nothing but stress, worry, and anxiety. We all are aware that becoming physically and emotionally withdrawn is dangerous because you start terminating relationships, cutting off people who care about you, and your communication becomes shorter and shorter with those around you, including those you work with.

The next thing you know, you have become codependent on negativity, guilt, stress, anger, and shame to survive because you have convinced yourself that you need things to live your daily life.

You feel as if you can't survive without these negative emotions because you feel like this is your world. You have now sentenced yourself to this for life. That is not actually your reality, but you believe it is, so you can no longer thrive or survive without negativity.

Just like an abusive or toxic relationship, you never leave it. You stay in the toxicity, and it is just like a hamster in a wheel, some people will just keep going round and round, never leaving the situation because they believe that is their life.

Eventually, you are going to start attaching yourself to things that are unhealthy, including people, habits, and relationships, and this will become normal to you because you have isolated yourself in a world of negativity and loneliness.

So, when you do start to interact with people, you only expect negative reactions and experiences. This is why you need to get out of the house and encounter other people, engage with different types of people, and do not isolate yourself from the world. Once again, this is only going to add to your stress.

Chapter 11. How to Control Your Anger

We are all human beings, and we are all going to have good and bad emotions, and negative emotions are just a part of us being human. The key is to have a positive way to express them because you definitely do not want to hold them in because they can end up causing you depression, anxiety, and all types of other issues.

Exercising management of your emotions, impulses, unhealthy desires, the way we speak, and our reactions to other people show that we are aware of our actions and responses. It demonstrates that we are able to be calm in difficult situations, which results in more productive and healthy relationships with family, friends, and co-workers.

So just make sure you are aware of and try to manage your emotions, do not let them control you. As long as you are able to manage them to the point where they do not take over you or control the way that you function in your everyday life, you should be okay.

Anger is a feeling we experience every day at random times, merely seeing someone cut in line when you have been standing for almost an hour can make you lose your calm. This is where we all differ.

Some individuals may get angry for a brief moment before regaining their calmness. For others, they might go completely out of control. This is why it is necessary to understand how angry you are in any situation.

Your anger is a potential cause of stress in your life.

Despite some of the issues with anger, it also offers some benefits to you. If you're in doubt, go through the next section.

Benefits of Anger

It Gives You a Sense of Control

When you get so angry and become confident enough to tell an individual off, then you get a feeling of being powerful. Although this may not be true, your anger at that moment makes it possible for you to become forceful and assertive. It allows you to be in charge if only for that brief moment.

People Respect Anger

As a form of response, people tend to respect your decisions when you're angry. The reason is that others assume that you are standing up for yourself when making these decisions. It is you being confident and assertive in a manner that prevents others from taking advantage of you.

You Get Positive Results

I'm sure this won't be a surprise to you. When you're angry, you usually get the results you want. If you portray yourself as the nicest person with people-pleasing habits, people tend to trample on your boundaries and ignore your decisions.

This doesn't apply when you're angry. At this point, you become intimidating and willing to confront others to get what you desire.

It Gives the Assumption that You are Working on Your Stress

There is usually a situation that triggers your stress. When you get angry, it is a response that promotes the assumption that you're channeling your energy toward resolving this situation. Anger prompts you to take action and quickly solve the problem at hand, even though forcefully.

Despite these benefits that make anger appealing, there are more adverse effects of this response. Understanding these negative sides of anger will make it easy to understand why you need to control it.

Problems with Anger

It Becomes Difficult to Make Friends

Developing a strong bond with others becomes a problem when you give in to your anger with ease. This lack of friendship makes things more challenging when you need to rely on your support system to overcome stress.

You Tend to Hurt Those Around You

This is one of the ways anger makes it difficult to build an effective support system. While you may be the most fun person to be around when you're calm, your anger might be destructive. You can end up physically or mentally abusing the ones you love and promoting conflict in the home due to this anger.

It Promotes Destructive Habits

Smoking, overeating, and drinking are some of the behaviors that you may adopt due to anger. Regardless of the reason, which is often in a bid to calm down, these behaviors have a negative impact on your health.

- The effect of anger on your stress levels

- Is there a right time to express anger?

Keeping your Temper in Check

Have you ever tried punching a wooden door just for fun? You feel the pain in your knuckles when taking this action. On the other hand, it is possible to punch through the same door when you lose your temper without feeling any form of pain.

This is why you need to learn to keep your temper in check.

Engaging in Anger Management Exercises

Anger management exercises are techniques that can assist you in remaining calm when you find yourself in stressful situations. There are numerous anger management exercises that you can try when you notice yourself getting angry. Here are some of the exercises that can help:

Progressive Muscle Relaxation

When you are getting angry, or under stress, one of the clear signs is muscle tension. Once you notice this sign, it is essential that you use progressive muscle relaxation exercises to maintain your calmness.

Applying this technique is straightforward. It requires you to focus on one muscle group of the body and then relaxing it. As soon as you relax this muscle group, you move on to another. You can start the process from the muscles in your toes and work your way to the head or the other way around.

This process will help you maintain your calmness just before you lose control.

Don't be Idle

This is merely a way to tell you to engage in regular exercises. This is important if you want to get effective anger management results or reduce stress. There is no shortage of physical activities to engage in when you're trying to control your anger.

You can take a walk, joy, or go for a ride on your bicycle. This will make it possible to overcome your anger.

Identifying Your Anger Triggers

Many people don't know the things that easily irritate them, which makes it challenging when dealing with their anger. There are specific triggers that are sure to make you lose your cool. Learning these triggers is an excellent way to prevent anger from taking control of your life.

All you need to do here is take some time to reflect on past instances in which you lost control. There are certain events you recall always makes you get angry. This event is one of your triggers.

There are also certain situations that you subconsciously avoid. These are undoubtedly some situations that quickly get you angry. Some individuals avoid walking past the desk of a particular coworker because they always do something annoying when they do. Others avoid driving to work because they aren't patient enough to wait in traffic.

Stop Replaying a Past Event Continuously

Some events make you angry, which you can resolve. It is common for individuals to engage in a process known as ruminating or dwelling. This involves repeating that same situation over and over in your head.

The problem with this action is that you make it easier for your anger to linger longer than necessary. This, in turn, causes your anger level to rise more than necessary. You must stop this process and move past such incidents.

Changing your perspective is one way to move on with ease. Is there any positive side to such a situation?

Learning to Listen

The problem with anger is that it clouds sound judgment. Situations that shouldn't have lasting consequences become significant issues because you keep exhibiting the jumping conclusion bias. You keep making assumptions without any substantial evidence to prove it.

You need to stop. Once you can stop yourself, then also make it a habit to listen to others in an argument. This is the only option available if you want to resolve the situation amicably with the right responses.

You don't have to make rash decisions; you can choose to take a walk to clear your head. This will help you respond better to the conversation.

Setting Expectations to Help in Remaining Calm

Why is it so easy to get angry when standing in line to purchase on a regular day, but you remain calm when waiting in line to get Black Friday deals? The reason is simple. You already expect the situation you find yourself in during the latter.

This is an excellent tip that can help you overcome your anger. You need to set appropriate expectations. Your anger may often be due to unrealistic expectations you set for the world around you.

If you expect others to be nice to you because you're nice to others, then you'll be surprised by what is to come. In your interaction with others, you tend to judge them based on your expectations. It is easy to become frustrated and angry when others don't meet up with these expectations.

In creating realistic expectations, the first step is to understand that people see things from a different perspective. It implies that the things they prioritize will differ from yours.

There are some questions that you can ask yourself to help you determine if you have realistic expectations. These include:

- Do you think you will miss the train or bus someday?

- Do you believe that a neighbor may decide to play loud music that will interfere with your work?

- Have you considered the possibility of your laptop crashing when you need it the most?

- Do you think of a day when you will be out of your job?

- Do you expect a loved one to disappoint you at some point?

These are simple questions that can help you set realistic expectations. In truth, you may never experience some of these situations in your lifetime. At the same time, if you give a straight 'No' as your answer to more than one of these questions, then you may have unrealistic expectations.

If you fall into this category, then you are likely losing yourself to anger because of the expectations you have of the world. To prevent this, you must accept that there are things that are beyond your control. It is also essential you prepare for these situations.

Most people prepare for a time when they don't have a job to go to. This is why they set aside a specific amount to put into a savings account. No one wishes for this situation, but everyone expects it to happen sooner or later.

Working on Your Short Fuse

What exactly is a short fuse? To identify this, you must determine how quickly you react when faced with a frustrating or unpleasant situation. If it only takes a few seconds or minutes for you to lose your calm, then you have a significant problem on your hands.

So how do you work on this short fuse? There is a way to achieve this goal that I will introduce to you. This is through this method known as "paradoxical intention."

Paradoxical intention refers to a process in which you face your fears or problems head-on. In this case, this implies putting yourself in situations that promote your anger and stress. This can help in extending your fuse, developing patience, and overcoming anger.

Various situations can induce an anger response. Standing in line for too long can be one of these situations. Another situation is dealing with a salesperson who lacks the experience to respond to you swiftly.

To achieve the goal of extending your fuse, then if you find yourself in a position to choose between two lines to join, pick the longest line. Since you regularly get frustrated and angry waiting in line, then you can work on your fuse by doing this frequently.

The same applies to dealing with an inexperienced salesperson. Make it a habit to pick the newest employee to help with your purchases. This will help you develop more understanding and patience.

Anticipate Various Anger-Provoking Situations and Rehearse Your Responses

This is something you should plan for when setting your expectations. You should expect to find yourself in a situation that will make you lose your temper. How do you get over such cases?

Preparing for such situations can have positive results. This preparation gives you a chance to evaluate a situation beforehand. Anger is a rapid response that doesn't give you enough time to perform proper evaluation and assessment.

Anticipation is crucial if you are to overcome this anger response. This is possible if you know the potential situations that can cause you to get angry. Working with these triggers in mind is your only option.

You are going to be coming up with various sentences that you'll say to prevent you from losing your temper. Examples of such situations can be an interaction with a coworker who doesn't try to work with other members of the team. This is one cause of disagreements in the workplace.

While rehearsing and choosing the right words to say, you should also expect the other person to get angry. Replay the scenario numerous times in your head and visualize how you can handle it without it escalating. This will better prepare you for real-life situations and help you get by without getting angry.

Another way to do this is to mimic a character you love. There are numerous TV shows that you can teach you a thing or two about anger management. These characters often engage in self-talk that helps them remain calm when they find themselves in such unpleasant situations.

Do you know any character that you can copy to help you remain calm? What will they say in such situations?

Find Humor in Anger Provoking Situations

When managing anger and stress, you can't undermine the importance of humor. Finding humor in situations that trigger your anger can help you minimize the effect of the situation. Laughing at past mistakes or your current situation is a way to eliminate the anger and stress that come with these situations.

Another alternative is to read books that contain humor. Make these books about the lives of others. This makes them relatable and promotes a feeling of acceptance in you.

Talking to friends can help. Seek out those friends who have a way to find humor in everything. The chances are they will find something absurd in your situation to make you laugh about it. This can be an excellent way to lose the anger that comes with the situation.

To simplify your task, you must make humor a part of your life. That means developing a sense of humor. As you maintain it, you find out that you can easily rely on it when you find yourself in overwhelming, stressful, and anger-inducing situations.

Chapter 12. How to Manage Interpersonal Interactions

Applying mindfulness to interpersonal interactions will open your eyes to how people are really not all that different at the end of the day. Just as how you have been shaped by your beliefs and childhood experiences, so have other people. You'll realize that labels, such as unintelligent or stupid, are simply a matter of mind and other such people simply haven't been exposed to the things that you have been to.

All in all, interpersonal mindfulness will make your world better and will also help you give the gift of mindfulness to those around you.

Patterns

Your beliefs have a lot to do with your relationship patterns and are formed in pretty much the same way. Your patterns are simply the behaviors you learned when you were little by modeling the actions of your parents. While the specific behavior might be different, emotionally the response is the same when your triggers are hit.

For example, if your parents simply didn't handle conflict well and deflected everything, odds are that you're going to end up doing the same thing. When you get into an argument with someone close to you, do you distract yourself by doing something else and avoid talking about the issues even when pressed? Do you then bring it up at the worst possible moment with the intention to hurt?

This is simply your way of avoiding the problem. Notice that you need not enact the exact action your parents used to enact but that the intention behind the action is the same. As with everything, communication comes down to intention. Conflict could further trigger unpleasant memories for you, and this results in you enacting further patterns.

Keep doing this long enough and you'll end up living between one pattern and the next, unable to break out of this vicious circle. So, why form such patterns form in the first place? Well, a lot of it has to do with how we learn when we're kids. As children, we're utterly helpless and are completely dependent on our parents for everything.

This leads us to model them in pretty much every aspect of our lives. Consider a child who boldly states that her father is the strongest man in the world or that her mother is the most beautiful person in the world. Such statements reflect the extent to which we worship and model our parents.

The problem is that our parents are people as well and as much as they love you, they have their own lives going on. They have their own worries, and this can lead to them setting a bad example for you. The end result is a pattern formed in your mind which continues to exert itself well into your adulthood.

The reason I'm delving into this is to clarify that everyone's parents screw up. It is unrealistic to expect a person to be a perfect parent and you should certainly not expect this from your parents or blame them for not being so. Ultimately, they did their best with what they had, and you can't ask for much more than this.

Blaming your parents for your patterns is a lot like traveling back into the past and regretting your actions. In this case, such reminiscence is even more worthless because the actions weren't even yours. Learn from their mistakes and move on. Don't make those mistakes with your kids, if you have any, but recognize that one day your kid is going to read this book and recognize your toxic patterns in their behavior.

This is part of the human condition, so accept it as it is and simply focus on doing your best, like your parents did. The first step to take is to recognize the qualities of mindful interpersonal interaction.

Qualities

Any relationship, no matter how bad it is, can be improved by applying these qualities of communication to it. Some of this will seem obvious, but if it's that obvious, why are you reading this book? Applying these methods and knowing them intellectually are two different things. Seek to apply these qualities as much as possible, and again, don't worry about doing them perfectly.

The reward lies in trying, not in achieving a perfect score.

Openness: Openness starts with a beginner's mind. Adopt an attitude of curiosity about what the other person is telling you and never assume you know what they're going to say. This way, you'll actually listen to them and be able to respond appropriately. Reviewing your intentions through the checklist of psychological biases will help as well since these might be clouding your judgment with regards to the person you're talking to.

Empathy: Walk a mile in their shoes. Empathy isn't just about acknowledging the other person's point of view or feelings; it is meshing it together with yours. Too many people harm themselves in the name of being empathetic.

Think of it this way: If you're down to your last dollar and someone asks you for one, there is no compulsion for you to lend your money, no matter how pressing their need is. Popular culture presents this as an act of great charity, but you should never place yourself in a disadvantageous position just to elevate someone else. The other person isn't asking that of you, so don't give it.

Compassion: Just like with empathy, compassion is both an intrapersonal and interpersonal quality. When interacting with someone, place your intention as being the reduction of suffering in the other person's mind. Seek to bring them to ease.

Now, you don't need to pity them when doing this but merely adopting this mental attitude will ensure you view things in a more rounded manner and take all viewpoints into account. If they are in genuine pain, try to understand the suffering they are going through and seek to reduce their burden. Again, do not disadvantage yourself when doing this since this is not the intention of compassion or empathy. Do whatever you can, as best as you can do it.

Loving kindness: It might sound ironic to hear this, but you will find it a lot easier to offer loving kindness to a stranger than to a difficult family member. This is because your family is the one that knows you inside and out, and you know them in the same way. You see all of their imperfections and weaknesses.

We often fall into the trap of looking at our loved ones from the perspective of what isn't there instead of acknowledging what is present. This leads us to seek conflict with them, even if our intentions are good. So, practice sending loving kindness to everyone you interact with and give them the gift of your love at all times.

Joy: Closely related to the transmission of loving kindness is the transmission of joy. Wish for the other person to experience this as they go about their lives. A good aid to enabling this feeling is to imagine them growing up through childhood and getting all of the things they wanted. Sounds a bit sappy, I know, but set your intention to transmit this and you'll marvel at how much better your relationships become, whether with a stranger or a loved one.

Equanimity: You didn't think you were going to escape this, did you? This is a book about mindfulness, after all! Equanimity, when viewed through the perspective of communication, is you realizing that whatever happens, the other person is going to do what they're going to do. Either way, it is not your job to mold their actions or generate results for them. You cannot change them, and they are perfect as they are. So, treat everyone as if they are perfect.

The six qualities will go a long way to improving the quality of your relationships and also your communication. If you apply them, you'll find that you'll be far more hesitant to fire off an irate email or snap back at someone. Mindfulness in everything will bring better results, and communication is no different.

Aikido and You

In any mindfulness-based stress reduction program, you will encounter the concept of using the principles of Aikido to enhance your communication. Aikido is a Japanese martial art and it focuses not on attack but on bringing peace. Every technique taught within Aikido is aimed at deflecting attacks in such a way that the aggressor or defender is unharmed.

It is a deeply spiritual practice as well since your intention needs to be aligned before practicing it or using the technique on anyone else. You can apply the principles of Aikido to your communication during difficult times. Communicating with our family and loved ones is the hardest thing to do because emotions run wild.

Given our proximity to them, we expect them to read our minds and understand everything we're saying. Often this feeling is mutual. Some family members even use the excuse of you being family to be extra rude to you because you ought to accept them for who they are, and if you can't, that means you're not really family. This will cause massive guilt and unhappiness within you. So, in light of all this, adopting the Aikido framework of communication is a great idea.

- Align: When facing an attack, it is important to first align yourself instead of seeking to avoid or repel the attack. Our reflex reaction is to repel and return in kind, but this is counter to our aims of mindful communication. Instead, listen mindfully. Listen to not just the words but the emotion behind it. Why are they wounded? Why are they attacking you? If you can't understand it, ask them with empathy what they're talking about, so that you can help solve their issue.

- Agree: The next step is to find areas you both agree on. This would be on facts or with regard to emotions. If the argument is about money, you could agree with them by saying that even you're nervous about the lack of it or that you feel that certain things are unjustified spending, just like they do.

Do not agree with them just for the sake of it since this is just insincere and they will pick up on it. Do not blame them for anything and instead restrict the conversation only to yourself. Talk about how you feel and what you think is correct in their words. Don't make it about them.

• Redirect: This step is where you begin to move forward and ask them what they think a valid solution might be. How do they think this conflict should be resolved? Having established that both of you agree on something, seek to resolve differences. As always, practice empathy and equanimity at all times.

• Resolve: Agree upon a solution that works for both of you. Mind you, this need not be the final solution and you can agree to revisit the situation again down the road.

At all times when using this framework, be mindful of your own emotions and your body language. Often, adjusting your body language will help you adjust your emotions appropriately and you'll find that you'll de-escalate the situation. When looking at the other person, be mindful of their body language and always try to listen to the intent behind their words.

People are not wordsmiths, so often they'll say one thing but really what they're trying to tell you is something else. So, listen to the emotion behind their words and ask them for clarification in case you don't understand. At every step, make it clear that you're interested in a resolution.

Mindful communication is tough because so much depends on the other person and you cannot control how they'll respond. You might find that the other person is stubborn and will not move towards a resolution no matter how hard you try. In such cases, react with equanimity and simply walk away.

Chapter 13. How to Live a Mindful Day

Living a Mindful Life Each Day

Living a mindful life each day may be the finest technique to attain complete reassurance. Mindfulness will help you handle every situation that comes the right path, particularly if happen to get working together with any anxiety. Being focused on living mindfully forever might seem daunting; however, these mindful living ideas will make it seem far more a pleasant and sustainable life-long process. To begin living mindfully on a daily basis, try the subsequent.

1.Take a time-out

Today, a lot more than ever, everyone is busy. From as soon as we wake until we time for bed, there is a rush of activities including working, eating, socializing, communicating, traveling and connecting online websites. In all these busyness, you will find there's very real chance for getting exhausted, burning one's self out and feeling overwhelmed.

At times genuinely, it might seem as being a challenge being positive and confident in all activities. That is why it's important to take a moment-out daily.

Although time-outs usually are associated using the punishment which you give that you simply child website marketing naughty, going for a time-out being an adult will help clear your brain. A time-out is often a period that you stop everything so which you'll be able to subside enough to put the human brain in with a rejuvenating meditative state.

You usually take time-outs in various ways. The most popular technique is by deciding on a scenic walk that you'll be able to admire greenery and butterflies, as an example. Or you might spend some time with your garden, away from all of the machines and gadgets that you use on a regular basis.

2. Complete one task with a time

The busier we have been, the harder we've got to get things done. Due to this, people will spend a significant amount of time looking to figure out the best way to multi-task. Multi-tasking will permit one individual to produce a large amount of tasks inside a very short time period.

The downside to multitasking could it be makes it hard to reside inside the present. What's worse is that this could allow a person to finish a bit of everything, but rarely completes an entire task.

Multi-tasking causes it to be hard to achieve awareness and adds to the odds of committing errors.

Mindful living demands someone to work by completing one task at the time. You can try this by allocating a certain timeframe per task, and towards completing the work within that point period. Then you can progress around the next task. This technique causes it to be easier for you to definitely always remain present.

3. Avoid nuances and build relationships

Relationships today are suffering much more so compared to they did 2 decades ago. On top of working constantly, so many people are finding it progressively hard to speak together. Part from the concern is because they've got allowed nuances ahead inside approach to communication.

These nuances come inside kinds of an assortment of conveniences and gadgets we love on day after day. These include mobiles, tablets and pagers. It could possibly be tempting to check on the cellphone regularly in the event that any message will be inside space of a few minutes. However, if you happen to become close with someone, while you are spending some time together, checking your phone always might appear disrespectful as well as unfair.

By practicing mindfulness meditation techniques, you, in turn, become more mindful of behaviors that are certainly not acceptable. Therefore, living mindfully requires a person to get clear boundaries with regards to their mobile phones. As portion of such boundaries, when spending time with anyone that you value the slightest bit, a mindful person could get their phone definitely not sight, so that they can fully be present with the one else and thereby connecting with them.

Mindfulness could even allow that you realize the amount you might have stopped considering people once you meet with them so that you simply can correct this and treat people using a bit more respect.

4. Do not hightail it in the feelings

From childhood, many people are, in fact, taught how to use from what these are generally feeling. Boys are told that they must not cry after they get injured. Girls are told they are going to endure heartbreak, plus they may have to get strong. These are some with the simple techniques we, as individuals, deny ourselves the opportunity of having deeper feelings.

Mindfulness is centered on feeling what you happen to become feeling. It allows that you accept precisely what exactly is happening on your heart, and not ending up being lost and far from control for accomplishing this. Learning being with feelings really helps to take away the effectiveness of negative feelings; plus, it helps one to accept life's challenges and see things that they're really.

When one comes with a mindful personality, they're planning to spend a substantial level of quantity of time in meditation and communing with themselves about the deeper level. This will assist to manage all anxiety, and can even promote emotional stability. This means that, inside the long term, there will likely be no should get from feelings whenever you might have each one of the tools that you just simply have to face them at the same time.

5. Allow your head to travel

Part for being focused requires one to definitely keep their mind in order. This means that people will actively avoid allowing their brains to wander, as this could seem they're wasting time and allowing the minds of men to obtain a 'mind party' all on their own.

However, a mindful person enables their mind to wander inside the present moment because it is only through mind wandering that they may take advantage of any thoughts that may be hindering their progress in the way of life.

Allowing the mind to wander permits some imaginative thinking to consider place, as issues and emotions are identified, then handled or discussed.

6. Mindful folks are creative people

The more one practices mindfulness techniques in their daily lives, the higher they realize that they're opening the minds of males. Minds are ready to accept different viewpoints, ways to being and gratification. It might be declared mindfulness makes people more creative.

As mindfulness reveals your mind, it permits creative thoughts also to find their way through amongst your constant barrage of thoughts on the selection of subjects. When you link meditation to creativity, it is an easy task to comprehend how mindfulness might have this sort of positive effect.

In fact, creativity may be used as being a way of reach a meditative state. This could possibly be particularly helpful for those who experience difficulty attempting to find time when they could sit aside and focus on meditating. It is possible to meditate while carrying out a favorite creative activity like dancing, cooking as well as just randomly sketching. Your mind will wind down if you pour your time into something creative.

7. Look out for brand spanking new experiences

It is easy, as well as a little as reassuring, to obtain organized inside daily routine of life. When this kind of thing happens, it might be challenging to exist inside present because you're vulnerable to believe that you just already know everything how the actual is offering.

A person that is living a mindful everyday life is offered to new experiences, and also, can even find these new experiences sometimes. Mindful, everyone is adventurous because they always live inside present moment and, therefore, wish to ensure which it in fact is well worth the cost.

They do this by conquering their fears and feelings, and dealing with any negative emotions that they could have at the moment. They have a chance to step inside unknown, which in turn times, requires one to definitely release some state internet marketing they will often have been waiting on hold.

Mindful people learn to face new situations with courage, exuding a persona of confidence though they're not absolutely clear on the things they may be going to see. The results of all of this are they'll experience lower numbers of stress; they are going to have higher examples of energy in addition to their knowing of detail which will improve dramatically.

8. Meditate

Finally, mindful people meditate each day. You cannot certainly be a mindful person in case you do not take the time to sit with your notions through meditation. These two techniques are so closely interrelated that, indeed, one cannot exist with any other.

Meditation is a great stress reliever, and yes, it allows one to interact consciously, making use of the thoughts. It also features a range of mental and physical health advantages. Together with mindfulness, a person might enjoy improved mental health and also the inclusion of proper life coping skills so as in order to avoid being overwhelmed when life fails.

Meditation, inside sense, might be seen as restarting one's body each day, renewing it and preparing it to your tasks that it must be yet to address. Living a mindful life every single day will enable one to ensure that you just pay focus on our self, your heartaches and that you simply appreciate everything as part of your present.

Your life is comprised of many different actions, and bringing mindfulness to all of them will go a long way towards decreasing your overall stress. All of your activities may be varied in nature, but the most important ones happen to be eating, exercising and social connection.

Pretty much everything we do as human beings is centered around these three things. Even those who avoid exercise end up indulging in the other extreme of it, which is to say that they rest all time. Mindfulness isn't about doing something as much as it is about achieving a balance between extremes. Ultimately, this is how the world is designed and, to remain in balance, existing between extremes is what a balanced and mindful life is all about.

Mindful Eating

I touched upon the practice of mindful eating at the beginning of this book when we looked at a different way of eating almonds. Food is such an integral part of our lives, yet we treat it with very little care. The preparation and consumption of food is often treated as a chore and we very rarely think about food as fuel for our bodies.

Mindful eating starts right from the moment you go grocery shopping. I do mean grocery shopping, as in buying raw ingredients and then cooking them into meals. I do not mean visiting your nearest fast food restaurant or searching for something that can be microwaved into something barely edible.

Processed foods and chemical additives have ruined our palettes to the extent that we do not even taste real food anymore. When you first switch to a whole food diet, you'll notice that you won't be able to taste a lot of the food you eat. This is because the flavors present in processed food are raised to an unhealthy degree and these foods are full of sugar. The net result is that your taste buds have been dulled and they need stimulation in order to figure out what it is you're eating.

When shopping, take your time to look at the different colors of food available. Marvel at the differences in texture, size and shapes of each ingredient. I'm not advocating converting to veganism or anything of the sort. Ultimately, everything we eat is food and this includes animals as well. Whether this is fine with you or not is up to your beliefs. Your aim should be to eat as balanced a diet as possible and this means including food from different food groups and blending as many colors into your food as possible.

This is a neat trick to figure out how balanced your diet is actually. The more varied the texture and colors in your food, the better the odds are that you're hitting your nutritional needs. Isn't it marvelous how nature has given us this easy way of determining this without needing to walk around with a calculator all the time?

As you prepare your food, infuse it with love and wish for it to provide nutrition and life to all those who consume it. When cooking, notice how the texture of the food changes and how all these diverse ingredients come together under heat to form a single dish. I'm not trying to get you to become a chef here, but the way raw ingredients come together to form a whole really is a miraculous process.

Where is your mind when you're eating your food usually? Probably on the TV or distracted with something else. Mealtimes are treated as a chore in most households and this really is a shame. Even if the whole family comes together for a meal, the objective isn't to enjoy the food, it is to talk about our day and to settle any lingering issues.

Take the time to notice what your food really tastes like and how it feels in your mouth. Acknowledge that this food is going inside you to fuel you and is a key contributor to your health. In modern society, we have a truly terrible relationship with food. Thanks to the rise of social media, our diets are under intense scrutiny and lots of food groups are demonized.

Some eat only carbs, and some eat only fat. Some claim juicing is the best and there's something called the fruit-based diet as well. Understand that all food is food. It doesn't matter what you eat as long as it is as naturally sourced as possible and that you eat it in the right quantities. Even junk food has its place, since eating the occasional burger will help you feel better.

Ultimately, this is what food is supposed to do. Make you feel good about living. Seek to achieve a state of balance with your food and it will return the favor to you via good health.

Mindful Exercise

Exercise can be summarized as you simply needing to move. You should always aim to be physically active and this is quite a challenge in today's world. If you had told someone 200 years ago that we would build special places just to run and exercise, they would likely have laughed at you. Well, the gym is a necessary part of our lifestyles these days.

Exercise need not be confined to just the gym; you can perform it outdoors as well. Yoga is a great form of exercise and you'll realize the greatest benefits of yoga when you perform and practice it as a group. Research has shown that exercise of any sort helps combat all sorts of health-related diseases. This doesn't refer to a single disease or type of exercise, mind you. All exercise is beneficial to stave off almost every single disease.

When choosing a program of exercise, pay special attention to your intention behind working out. Your intention should inform the activity. If your goal is to merely stay healthy, then working out outdoors, either in the morning or during dusk, is extremely beneficial. If your intention is something more specific, such as increasing your muscle mass and so on, then a gym is the ideal place for that.

When working out, place your full attention on your movements. There is a social element to exercise and most people visit the gym to catch up with their buddies or check out the other people working out. Whether you choose to indulge in this sort of thing or not, remember that your primary goal is to exercise. It isn't to socialize. Once you're done, do whatever it is you want, but when exercising, place your full focus on executing your movements correctly.

A lot of injuries sustained in the gym are due to either inattention or due to the wrong intention. What I mean by wrong intention is when someone tries to lift a weight that is too heavy for them because they're trying to show off in some manner. Mindful exercise will remove the risk of this ever happening.

Another key point to remember, and this ties in with mindfulness, is to pay attention to just what you're doing. It is tempting to look around and compare yourself to others working out, but this is a useless exercise since it only removes you from a mindful state. Above all else, listen to your body and respect its needs.

Do not overtrain or think that you need to push yourself. Regular exercise puts you in greater touch with your body since you'll be able to feel it changing in shape as you get fitter. Examine your body prior to working out for signs of fatigue. One of the things you'll get used to is telling the difference between soreness and injury and that pain isn't always a bad thing.

The best way to think of exercise is to keep moving as much as you can. Most of us work sedentary jobs these days and rarely get the opportunity to exercise our muscles. So, walk when you have the chance and lift things at home as much as possible. Try to end your day with a walkout in nature as this will calm you and give you a chance to meditate as well.

You do not need to aim to look like a supermodel or aim to get as ripped as some bodybuilders. The point is to be healthy. Understand that there are different forms of health and that everyone's bodies are different. Focus on your own goals and tune out the noise that the fitness industry sends your way. You don't need a fancy diet or a fancy workout routine in order to get fit.

Just listen to your mind and body and follow what they tell you. You already know what to do.

Social Connection

Human beings are social creatures. Everything we do is centered around the fact that we need to connect with one another. We've built vast networks and information highways for precisely this purpose. Mindfulness practices help you realize how interconnected everything is.

You will realize that everything in this world is created and connected to one another. Look at how the ecosystem exists. There is a food chain, and this has a circularity to it, with the animal on top eventually nourishing the thing at the bottom. Life is circular and everything is connected.

As you forge connections with other people, practice the eight pillars of mindfulness. Listen with your whole being instead of simply waiting for your turn to speak. Nurture and care for some form of life in your personal time. You need not go out and start making babies, but even a simple act of caring for a plant or a pet will bring greater meaning to your life.

Research shows that people need to take care of one another and need to love and be loved. Older people who live in assisted living facilities live longer when they need to take care of a plant or a pet. Life ultimately sustains life.

Some people display an aversion to social connection thanks to past trauma. If you're one of those people, you should explore this resistance during your sitting meditation. Shine a light on it and remember to not label or judge it. Simply observe it and you'll unearth the root cause of it.

As with everything else, set your intention to form meaningful social connections on an emotional level. Social media has distorted what it means to be social. Having thousands of Facebook friends does not mean you're social. You probably wouldn't recognize the majority of those people if you saw them on the street. Interacting with people online and tweeting at them isn't being social.

The online world distorts what humanity is by amplifying the extreme. Social media companies actively engineer this since outrage is what drives engagement. Simply put, the angrier and more volatile you get, the more you're going to use their platform. Add to the fact that human beings have a negative bias during the best of times, and it's easy to convince yourself that hatred is increasing and that the world is going to hell.

Disconnect from all forms of social media right now and go dark for about a week. This might be impractical for some, so schedule two fifteen-minute periods per day to answer emails and check out the latest social media stuff. Disconnect completely from the news and choose to move on with your life instead. You'll be surprised to note that birds still chirp, and squirrels still come running at you when you give them food.

Understand the real meaning of social connection by interacting mindfully with those around you and seeking as many in-person relationships as possible. Try to get to know people as best as you can and understand that you're going to rub some people the wrong way. You'll also be met with strange glances when you tell people that you don't have a social media profile, but that's easy to deal with.

Focus on connection and not on being "social." A lot of your problems and stress will automatically melt away.

Rest

By rest, I'm not talking about just sleep. I'm referring to periods during the day when you simply lounge about and do nothing in particular. I'm also telling you that you need to schedule these as meticulously as you would schedule your meditation sessions.

Rest, or lounging about, is one of the best gifts you can give yourself. It allows your mind to go wandering about and pick up whatever it wants to. Much like how the occasional piece of junk food energies you, rest will help you recover and refresh your mind from the day's proceedings.

Your brain will tell you how much rest it needs for the most part. Simply listen to it and follow its instructions. Nothing could be simpler.

Conclusion

Having confidence is about being able to put one step in front of the last without doubting that step. It's about knowing that what you do in your life is your choice and knowing that no one else can make those choices for you. Don't live by other people's standards. Create your own.

The most important thing that you can take with you from this book is the following, which is based on a practice called mindfulness:

Yesterday is gone – You cannot change it and it doesn't count anymore.

Tomorrow has not yet arrived – worrying about it won't help it to be better.

This moment in life is all that you have.

It's perfectly astute and correct to assume that this moment within your life may be all that you have. Thus, learn to embrace it and stop feeling bogged down by other people's judgment of you. If you made mistakes in the past, don't make them in this moment and don't waste this moment by letting your thoughts drag you into the past. If you can make things right with people by apologizing, do so. If you can't, learn from the mistake and don't make it again.

Depression can go away, but you have to understand that a thought that you have today isn't important in the overall picture of life. If you waste this moment on negative thoughts, you go into the next moment with negativity already there in your life. If you fill this moment with a positive action, you reinforce your value and you move forward into the next moment as a better person than you were a moment ago. Thus, it follows that building up your confidence should be done moment by moment. I made a friend a cup of coffee because I knew that she was lonely. It made her feel better. It made me feel better. Small gestures that take selfish thought out of the picture help to build up positivity that helps to pull you out of the pits of depression. I helped a lady with her shopping because she was older and struggling. When you give, give with no expectations of return because that's the kind of giving that helps you to build up your confidence in yourself. You do things because you know they are positive things to do. You don't do them for thanks or for something given in return. When you incorporate giving into your everyday life, it's a positive reminder to yourself that you have value.

It is also important to avoid a life of isolation and loneliness, as this will only feed your fears and anxiety. Instead, cultivate positive connections with people who care, go out, make friends, and appreciate that you are important. If you have faced rejection in the past, try to keep that where it belongs, in the past, and forge ahead. Share your anxieties with those who love you and view yourself as a problem solver in life as well.

This will help reduce your vulnerability and give you a platform to deal with your problems.

Let's hope this book was informative and able to provide you with all of the tools you need to achieve your goals, whatever it is that they may be. Just because you've finished this book doesn't mean there is nothing left to learn on the topic, and expanding your horizons is the only way to find the mastery you seek.

Now that you have made it to the end of this book, you hopefully have an understanding of how to get started overcoming stress once and for all as well as a strategy or two, or three, that you are anxious to try for the first time. Before you go ahead and start giving it your all, however, it is important that you have realistic expectations as to the level of success you should expect in the near future.

While it is perfectly true that some people experience serious success right out of the gate, it is an unfortunate fact of life that they are the exception rather than the rule. What this means is that you should expect to experience something of a learning curve, especially when you are first figuring out what works for you. This is perfectly normal, however, and if you persevere, you will come out the other side better because of it. Instead of getting your hopes up to an unrealistic degree, you should think of your time spent improving your mental health as a marathon rather than a sprint which means that slow and steady will win the race every single time.

In conclusion, it's a great idea to look at yourself in the mirror every morning and affirm yourself. Say to yourself things like, "I am a resilient person who can deal with and overcome whatever scenario comes my way today." Hear yourself declare it loudly and let it become your conviction every day. When faced by anxious moments, fight hard and resist the temptation to give in. Anxiety is not a chronic disease; you can overcome it and will overcome it.

www.ingramcontent.com/pod-product-compliance
Lightning Source LLC
Chambersburg PA
CBHW070650250726
48662CB00001B/46